EMANCIPATION OF EIGHT GENERATIONS

To The ~~████████~~ Family
from
James O. Hill, Sr.

Jan 16 – 2006

EMANCIPATION OF EIGHT GENERATIONS

The Chambers Family Treasure

James O. Hill, Sr.

Foreword by Levi Henry, Jr.

Hill Family Enterprise
Fort Lauderdale, Florida

Emancipation of Eight Generations: *The Chambers Family Treasure*, by James O. Hill, Sr.

Publisher: Hill Family Enterprise
Editor: Dale H. Rosenberg
Development Editor: Dr. Romando James
Media Developmental Editors: Eva M. Taylor and Bernadette Hence, Ed.D.
Marketing Manager: Oswaldo Casco
Production Editor: Lourdes Rodriguez
Media Production Editor: Levi Henry, Jr.
Production Coordinator: Joseph Valmond
Graphic Design: Peak Print & Marketing, Inc.
Marketing and Promotion: Peak Print & Marketing, Inc.

Printed in the United States of America

For more information contact:
Hill Family Enterprise
P.O. Box 1448
Fort Lauderdale, FL 33302
jamesohill22@yahoo.com

For permission to use material from this text or product, contact us by:
• telephone: (954) 583-6452
• fax: (954) 316-4986
jamesohill22@yahoo.com

Library of Congress Cataloging-in-Publication Data

LCCN: 2005904904

Hill, James O., Sr.
    Emancipation of Eight Generations / James O. Hill, Sr.

ISBN 0-9755181-0-0

Dedication

To my mother, Ethel Hill, in recognition of her
loyalty and devotion to her family and relatives,
as well as to her lifelong willingness to always
serve the needs of others before addressing her own.

To the Chambers Family, our friends
and acquaintances of
Austin, Texas
Fort Lauderdale, Florida
the United States of America
and throughout the world.

DECEMBER 1830 to DECEMBER 2004

The growth and development of one very large
Black family from Texas spanning 173 years.

Contents

Illustrations

Figures

Maps

Tables

Foreword

By Levi Henry, Jr.,
Owner and Publisher of the
Westside Gazette
Fort Lauderdale, Florida
(Broward County's oldest and largest African American-owned newspaper)

Few, if any, would feel more honored or more privileged than I to introduce James O. Hill, Sr., whom I have known and been associated with since 1968. I was commissioned as a committee of one by the Boys Clubs of Broward County to officially meet and welcome Mr. Hill, his wife Eva, and his daughter to Fort Lauderdale on that hot May day. I suppose I can never forget it. Emergency circumstances confronting his family immediately upon their arrival here forged a close relationship between our two families that has flourished through the years. Although he and I had many opportunities to become acquainted by way of our years of working together on behalf of the City of Fort Lauderdale and while executing our community relations responsibilities in neighborhoods throughout the city, it was through our interactions with our families that I really came to know and to appreciate the kind of person Jim is. His sense of dedication, loyalty, and service to his family, friends, and the citizens of Fort Lauderdale made him a legend in his own time.

James O. Hill is well-traveled. The son of the Reverend and Mrs. William "Will" Hill, James was born and raised in Austin, Texas, educated at San Francisco City and State Colleges, Howard, New York, and Nova Southeastern Universities. With a degree in sociology, his services were sought by the National Boys Clubs of America through New York University. He was initially appointed Social Recreation Director for the Boys Clubs of Newark, New Jersey. Jim was elevated to Acting Club Director in 1968 before moving to Broward County, where he became the first professional Black director in the state of Florida. In this capacity, Jim influenced the lives of over twenty thousand boys and girls of all ethnic and racial backgrounds.

On October 28, 1971, the Fort Lauderdale City Manager's Office announced the appointment of Hill as Administrative Assistant, the first Black to be appointed to a key administration post in the City's history. On October 2, 1973, he was appointed Assistant City Manager, the first Black to be appointed to such a position by any city in Broward County and the second in the state of Florida. To fully prepare himself for this position, Hill earned a Master's in Public Administration.

While maintaining his duties and responsibilities as Assistant City Manager and to allow the administration to utilize his sociological skills in the involvement of citizens and organizations in achieving the City's mission of becoming the best city of its size in the United States by 1994, Hill was appointed Director of Community Relations in 1989, but soon became Business Retention and Expansion Manager of the City in 1993 to assist with management of the City's new Economic Development Department.

The Fort Lauderdale Historical Society named Hill winner of the 1990 Byron Snyder Award presented annually by the society to the individual having made the most significant contribution to preservation of the City's heritage. He is pioneer organizer of the Fort Lauderdale/Broward Sistrunk Historical Festival, which has attracted over 150,000 people to Fort Lauderdale annually since 1980.

In recognition of his distinguished public service career and the valuable contributions made to the City of Fort Lauderdale, the City Commission publicly recognized and acknowledged these achievements and contributions on April 20, 1999, by selecting and honoring James Hill as Exemplary City Employee for 1999, the highest honor to be conveyed upon an appointed employee of the City. A plaque honoring Mr. Hill has been placed in the lobby of the Fort Lauderdale City Hall that will remain forever.

In his long career, James Hill developed a great interest in the American family, the Black family in particular. Viewing the family as an institution having a great impact on each of its members, his attention became focused upon his own family. He was reflective of the influence his grandparents, James Arthur Garfield Chambers and Marie Reese Chambers, had on his personal life and on the lives of other family members. He considered how family members survived as indentured servants and slaves and now as emancipated Blacks living in today's nonsegregated society forty-nine years after declaration of the 1954 U.S. Supreme Court decision which ended segregation here in America. Telling the story of his family became a priority, a must for the history of Blacks.

Emancipation of Eight Generations: The Chambers Family Treasure illustrates how one ordinary Black Texas family rose above overwhelming social barriers. Through extensive research James Hill discovered that their ancestral lineage was actually traceable through eight generations and that he is a fifth-generation member. Mr. Hill reveals how his interactions with members of the Reese and the Chambers families since his early childhood impacted his life and helped to prepare him for his successful career in Fort Lauderdale Municipal Government. Colorful and historical memories of his old St. John community in Austin, Texas, where he grew up, its segregated school, and its pioneers have also been included, along with fond memories and photographs of classmates and teachers of old Anderson High School, as a commemoration to those times.

A living testament to the legacy of the late Garfield and Marie Chambers, the author provides a fact-based and biographical profile of this incredible Black American couple by depicting the influence they exhibited on their community, friends, their own family members, and, especially, himself. Rarely has a family as big made an effort so great to become acquainted, even though they lived so far apart in place and in time. This author asks, "Why shouldn't a family be concerned about knowing even the smallest of its members?" He challenges his own family to become a stronger and more committed family. He urges all families to consider the challenge as well. According to Mr. Hill, he once heard his Grandmother Marie, "Big Momma," say that "a strong family stands on the rock of stability and the warmth of the love they are willing to extend to each other."

In 2001, James Hill considered retirement from municipal government, but, instead, chose to diversify. Promotion of this book is one of his many projects. I encourage you to read this book about family history and culture. You will reap from it, as well, the story of a young boy from Austin, Texas, who grew up and made history in Fort Lauderdale, Florida, by making things happen through government, in the way he knew best, in the style of The Chambers Family Treasure.

Prologue

I am here with a sincere desire to awaken the sensibilities to kindle the dormant fibers in the soul and to fire . . . racial patriotism by the study of . . . Negro Books. . . . We need a collection . . . of books written by our men and women. . . . We need in the coming dawn the man, who will give us the background for our future, it matters not whether he comes from the cloister of the university or from the name card file of the fields. We await his coming. . . .

Arthur A. Schomburg
Cheyney Institute, July 1913

In those rolling hills of Wilbarger Community, the snow-white cotton fields of Manor, and the St. John neighborhood of Austin, Texas, a new, freer man was born, one who was unhindered by tradition, restless and independent, endlessly optimistic, hard-working, and totally unafraid.

Following graduation from Anderson High School in Austin, Texas, in 1955, I was determined to go to college immediately, but had no money other than $38 I had earned cutting lawns that summer. With my parents' approval and the invitation from Aunt Mary and Uncle Ross Westbrook, I left home at seventeen years of age in search of a future.

California's call to me was urgent, and San Francisco became the frontier of my adult life. James and Lottie Caldwell, whom I had met shortly after my arrival in the Bay Area, showed great compassion by taking me into their home, becoming my godparents, and caring for me as though I were their own. Their people became my people. Wherever I would go, they followed. We became family for life.

College life at San Francisco City and State Colleges was as exciting as I always dreamed it would be. A simple part-time job at I. Magnin department store after class each day and on Saturdays provided a lifestyle for me that I had never known before, allowing me to buy my first car, cameras, new clothes, as well as to have friends and money to finance my own education and to have a real chance to grow up.

I searched for a future in San Francisco for almost three years but never found one. The United States Air Force took me to the Black Hills of Rapid City, South Dakota, for four years of active duty in the service of my country, from 1958 to 1962. The Dakotas were not for me either, though memorable beyond compare. Following my release from the military, I expanded my search to Washington, D.C., where I graduated from Howard University in 1964. Seemingly, my long search was finally nearing an end. Boys Clubs of Newark, New Jersey, recruited me to sign my first professional employment contract, an experience for which I had always longed.

I am now in the sixth decade of my life, a time of reflection and of taking a measure of my accomplishments toward the high goals of my youth and of my debts to those who guided and shaped my life. To the earliest traceable-known figure of our family roots, Miriah Reese, my great-great grandmother, I proudly confer my greatest honor. I am thankful to the Reese and the Chambers families, my friends, church, colleagues in government, as well as civic groups, through which I expressed my concerns for the brotherhood of man. Hence, *Emancipation of Eight Generations: The Chambers Family Treasure* is my own story, but part of theirs as well. Before and during my lifetime, many books and other publications had already been written about the Black struggle for survival and equal citizenship for Blacks here in the United States. I thought the time had finally come for me to write my own story of family struggle.

Looking back, in retrospect, Blacks have been living in the United States since 1619, when the people of African descent were brought to Jamestown, Virginia, approximately 384 years ago. At first, they were indentured servants, but, eventually, they were forced into legal slavery in 1691. They were emancipated more than two hundred years later, in 1863, and have lived ever since in a multicultural society where people of all races, by necessity, have been forced to live and to work together for the common good. This situation has not been too easy for some, but in spite of unusual barriers and difficulties, many Black families have done well to survive. In my opinion, the Peter Reese family and the James Arthur Garfield Chambers family of central Texas are remarkable examples of two such families. I am fortunate to be a member of both.

Jim Hill, looking back

Black leaders who both lived through and studied the social and the political trends of those turbulent years had suggested alternative strategies for resolving the many social and racial problems our country and its peoples had experienced during the past two centuries. Frederick Douglass, a Republican admirer and sympathizer, as I am, and foremost representative of the best efforts of Blacks to abolish slavery, was the first to advocate political involvement for them. His good friend and colleague, Booker T. Washington, opposed this approach, describing such strategy as unwise. The only way for the Black freedmen to build a house, a life, or a civilization, Mr. Washington had reasoned, was to begin at the bottom and work up. He considered political activity on the part of freedmen as trying to start from the top. According to Washington, both wealth and prosperity and trades and skills were the immediate first objectives Blacks should seek to silence agitation for citizenship rights. With time, Mr. Washington later relinquished his leadership role to W. E. B. Du Bois, who became the spokesman for the NAACP in 1911. Finally, Black leadership was provided by a string of folk heroes, such as Adam Clayton Powell, Jr., Thurgood Marshall, and Dr. Martin Luther King, Jr. I knew and praised each one of them.

Garfield and Marie Chambers were married in 1903 and immediately began raising their family. Garfield was primarily a farmer and sharecropper. However, he followed politics and kept current on political affairs by listening to the radio, reading newspapers whenever he could get them, and conversing with people of knowledge. He was deeply interested in American history and American heroes and leaders, both Black and White. Although impressed with the political scholars of the time, he always had a specific strategy of his own for achieving full freedom and citizenship as a child of emancipated slaves. Garfield and Marie shared the values and the visions of their enslaved forefathers that someday life would be better for them, as well as for their children and grandchildren. Adopting the general philosophy that Booker T. Washington had advocated and placing their full belief and faith in the hands of the Almighty God, Garfield and Marie went forth to create a legacy only a few others could match.

I was a senior in 1954 when the U.S. Supreme Court decision was passed declaring segregation unconstitutional altogether. In 1964, Black leadership in the United States was heading to a new phase. No one Black leader could speak for Blacks as a whole. This was the 1960s, and as a young, educated Black man, I thought the time was right for me to take a good look at myself and my family to see what we could do, ourselves, to further our own cause and to experience some of the good life as freedmen and women of today.

As the years passed, the yearning to know my family had begun to fester as never before. I began to seek new knowledge about our family roots and history. The more I learned about the family, the more I began to appreciate the important roles played by the late Mr. and Mrs. Garfield Chambers during their lifetimes that have contributed so much to the quality of life and freedom our families enjoy today.

Essential to understanding the growth and the development of the Chambers family was the creation of a historical and sociological framework by which to establish a reasonable perspective for viewing and analyzing our family group at different points in time. I have therefore identified three of the most significant historical landmark events in American Black history which best describe the conditions and the circumstances the Reese and the Chambers families had to overcome in order to survive and to achieve the goals they had established. Legalized slavery, the emancipation of slaves, and the 1954 U.S. Supreme Court decision declaring segregation unconstitutional each had a profound impact on our family and on the Black American dreams of other families as well.

Emancipation of Eight Generations is a nonfiction story detailing the history and the lives of my late grandparents, Mr. and Mrs. Garfield Chambers, son and daughter of former Black slaves who married, settled in Bastrop County, Texas, raised a family of twelve, and saw that family multiply and relocate to areas throughout the United States so rapidly that the family had almost become like strangers.

Emancipation of Eight Generations is more than a story about an outstanding Black family. It is a story about an incredible Black couple who, during sixty-three years of marriage, managed to raise and to educate their family of twelve. At the same time, they transitioned from an agrarian, sharecropper lifestyle in Bastrop County to become urbanite landowner citizens within the city of Austin, Texas. This was successfully accomplished throughout the years of the Great Depression and World War II, when times were hard and educational and job opportunities for Blacks in Texas were quite limited.

Garfield and Marie Chambers were among the pioneer settlers of Austin's St. John community, its community school, Fiskville, and Blacks Memorial Baptist Church, where I grew up as a child under their watchful and lovable guardianship.

My vision for writing this book came on August 3, 1987, while I was delivering the family's response address at the funeral of Marie Chambers. During my address, I began to reflect upon all the stories and the experiences that had been revealed to me by my grandparents from my childhood to their passing. It was as if my grandmother were revealing to me, as I stood there about to speak, the trials, tribulations, and hopes of a Black woman wanting to bring and to keep her family close together as always. With fond memories, I flashed back on her life as I remembered it and as she would have liked it told:

- her father and mother,
- sisters and brothers,
- nieces and nephews,
- Garfield Chambers, the man she married,
- their family of twelve,
- four generations of grandchildren,
- her memories of the past and visions of the future,
- her home,
- her church,
- the community,
- friends and contemporaries,
- deceased loved ones,

- her evaluation and understanding of being colored, Negro, African American, and, finally, Mrs. Marie Reese Chambers, a proud Black woman.

Following Grandmother Marie's passing, the family made a commitment to get to know each other better. Writing this book became part of that commitment. Join me, now, as I, James O. Hill, Sr., tell the story of the Reese and the Chambers families. Along the way, I will recount some personal events experienced with various members of this very large Black American family.

Acknowledgments

A special thanks to my coworkers and friends at the City of Fort Lauderdale, including Donna Deifer, Patricia Austin, Isabel Rincorn, Suzan Holmes, Wayne Bernard, and Lourdes Rodriguez, for their professional assistance and technical guidance in the production of this documentary enterprise. I am grateful to all of my relatives and friends for sharing and for providing their treasured photographs and other personal data required to complete this production. My cousin, the Reverend R.J. Reese, and his wife Iowa were especially inspirational to me. Cousin Helen Chambers Patterson convinced me to include photographs, while Gerri Nash and Raymond Westbrook encouraged me to finish this project at times when I felt like giving up. Cousins Jean and Rutherford Yates reassured me that I was capable of pulling this project together. It is what my sister Minnie; my wife Eva; my children, Eva, Jim, and Dudley, all expected of me because I am not a quitter.

Our cousin, Adel Scott, refreshed our memories of Fiskville School, St. John's first and only neighborhood school, its principal and faculty members by providing me with a copy of the school's last program report which she had kept since 1949. Regrettably, Adel passed away in June 1999 before the completion of this book.

Sherrie Mahoney and the city of Bastrop, Texas Chamber of Commerce assisted me greatly by providing maps and graphics which made it possible to show a geographic location of the Chambers family home in Texas. The Sayersville, Texas Historical Society has done extensive research on the Reese family, enabling me to reveal the true richness of the family's intriguing folklore and charm.

Photographic restoration was performed by Suncatcher Studios of Fort Lauderdale, Florida, by resurrecting and restoring photographs of the late Peter Reese and his mother, Miriah Reese (believed to have been taken during the late 1880s), to almost modern-day standards and quality.

Additionally, I was so lucky to have met Joshua Jenkins. Through his artistic genius and imaginative skills, Joshua depicted a symbolic evolution of the Garfield and Marie (Reese) Chambers family by the creation of our family tree in his own unique image.

Finally, deep gratitude is extended to Joseph Valmond and Michele Scanlan, Peak Print and Marketing, Inc., for their expertise in project management and graphic design; Dale H. Rosenberg, professional communication consultant, Dale H. Rosenberg Consulting, for her patience and expertise in guiding me through the intricacies of literary writing; and Bonnie Greene, reading teacher, Broward County Public Schools, for her assistance in creating the Student Handbook that will accompany this book when used as a teaching tool.

Grateful acknowledgment is made to all the foregoing relatives, friends, and professionals for helping to make my wish a reality.

Photographs

COURAGE OF A LIGHTNING GHOST

(EMANCIPATION OF EIGHT GENERATIONS)

Description of Photographs on the Cover

Photographs of the late Miriah Reese and her son Peter Reese, believed to have been taken during the late 1880s, which were discovered by a relative in the late 1960s and were restored in 1996, give a glimpse of the early dawning of the Reese side of the family.

Like a ghost from the deep shadow of her past, the photograph of the late Miriah Reese portrays the courage, stamina, and determination of a mixed breed slave mother who, like a flash of lightning, sparked the creation of her own American family linkage to eight generations.

The photograph of the late Reverend Peter Reese reflects the tradition of family and moral values he felt required to maintain in order to sustain his honor and pride as a freedman.

The Quest for Freedom in Early America

(A Philosophy of Citizenship)

The struggle for survival, freedom, and citizenship in early America by the Reese and the Chambers families dates back to the early 1800s. This was approximately 181 years after the first people of African descent were brought to Jamestown, Virginia, by a Dutch man-of-war ship.

Two major economic activities escalated slave trade between Africa and the New World. The first was the demand for cheap labor to harvest the sugar cane industries in the Portuguese- and Dutch-controlled areas. The second was the demand for laborers to harvest the tobacco industries in Virginia, as well as to harvest the corn and cotton industries in the south and southeastern areas of the United States. After the fall of Ghana, West Africa, the African chiefs, or kings, sold their war captives, those of their own people enslaved for whatever reason and those in debt who wished to barter for their future freedom. These situations alone resulted in the deportation of thousands of Black West Africans from Ghana to locations in the West Indies, Mexico, and the eastern and southeastern shores of the United States in the early to mid-1700s.*

The demographic patterns of slave migration to different cities in the United States were determined by the nature of employment opportunities being sought. Hence, industrial-minded people usually went to Detroit or Pittsburgh. Farmers and agricultural workers most often headed west or southwest (i.e., Louisiana or Texas). In his book *From Slavery to Freedom: A History of Negro Americans*, John Hope Franklin reported that the people of Ghana were agriculture- and trade-oriented people. They still are today.

By the eighteenth century, the Black population within the state of Virginia had grown at such an alarming rate that Virginians became apprehensive about having such large numbers of these people living among the Whites. Whites and Blacks were mixing, and a mulatto population emerged.

Blacks of Virginia were beginning to show signs of dissatisfaction with Whites and began to plot rebellions against their masters. They generally showed resentment against their status as slaves. An attempt was made to stop or, at least, to reduce the number of Blacks coming into the state when a bill seeking to prevent slave trade to foreign ports was introduced in Congress in 1790. Finally, on

---

* Ironically, on June 21, 2000, I coordinated the historical visit of His Majesty, F.A. Ayi, Symbolic King of Togo, West Africa, to Fort Lauderdale, Florida. His mission was one of reconciliation and healing among people. The king publicly apologized to African American citizens for the fact that some Africans had sold other Africans into slavery and had worked with European slave traders following the fall of Ghana. In spite of some questions a few individuals raised relative to the authenticity of Ayi's kingship, Fort Lauderdale Mayor Jim Naugle and I believed in and supported the purpose and the cause of his mission.

March 2, 1807, the law prohibiting African slave trade was passed. The peace that settled over the United States shortly after the War of 1812 made possible for a great westward movement, which saw a considerable number of Whites and Blacks migrate from the seaboard states to the western states, where a Cotton Kingdom was rapidly emerging.

The story of the Reese and the Chambers families originates with Miriah (maiden name unknown) and her parents. My review of important historical occurrences surrounding the rise and the fall of Ghana prior to the 1800s gives rise to the speculation that Miriah's parents may have been among the first Africans who were brought to Jamestown in the late 1600s (see map 1.1).

Miriah Reese

The settling of Missouri and the acquisition of Texas in 1845 are among the major events which somehow may have resulted in the relocation of Miriah's parents from Virginia to a location in Tennessee, where Miriah was born a slave around 1830. Miriah and her parents are believed to have remained in Tennessee for a number of years. Miriah was mulatto, with some Spanish features. Her fair-toned coloring is quite evident in her photograph. She later married a Reese (first name unknown), who was also a resident of the state.

As southern slave owners continued to indulge in slave trade and the splitting up of slave family members, those slaves who sought freedom fled from Tennessee into the northern and western states and Canada. The Underground Railroad aided many slaves to escape successfully to destinations often unknown. Miriah Reese and her husband migrated to Bastrop County, Texas (see map 1.2). Exactly how they got there, however, is unknown. Early after their arrival, Miriah gave birth to their son, Peter Reese. Evidence to the speculation that Miriah Reese and her husband were born in Tennessee is offered in the fact that the Twelfth Census Records of the United States in Bastrop County list Tennessee as their place of birth (see figure 1.1).

Peter Reese grew up in Bastrop County, where he met and married Lilia Baltimore at a very early age. Lilia had married her first husband, Plez Mitchell, soon after her arrival in Texas. To this union, two children, Margie and Sam, were born. Lilia married Peter Reese following the death of Plez Mitchell. She was thought to be in her mid- to late-thirties at the time.

Peter Reese

Unlike any of Peter's family, Lilia was able to give a personal account of how she and her sisters and brothers migrated to Texas from Missouri. She often related to her children and to her oldest grandchildren the story of her plight. According to the account she gave, she, her two sisters, Mary and Martha, and her two brothers, George and Bud, were among a group of freed slaves who traveled via a small mule-drawn wagon from the state of Missouri to a place in Texas called "Old Mill," located near the town of Magdilene. Lilia would often recount to a granddaughter

Lilia Reese at 110 years old

events that she remembered happening to the group while making the trip. Experiences such as having to drink water out of the wagon wheel ruts in the road were common for her and for her brothers and sisters, who managed to remain together as a family during those years of transition when many slave families were being separated through trade and other purchase transaction arrangements.

Marie Reese, Peter and Lilia's first child, was born on May 7, 1884. Marie Reese grew up rapidly, met and married James Arthur Garfield Chambers (known as Garfield), and had begun to raise her own family by early 1900. During this time, Jim Crow laws and customs supported all forms and degrees of racial segregation and discrimination in the United States. Nevertheless, the Chambers family somehow managed to survive and to flourish without exhibiting the deep resentment toward Whites as some might have expected they should. Marie and Garfield Chambers shared the belief commonly held by many Blacks prior to the Emancipation Proclamation, that is, that they must be hard-working and practical, God-fearing, obedient to law, self-respecting, and upright. They were eager to assume that if Blacks improved themselves individually by getting an education on the same level as Whites of their time, by developing usable occupational skills and by adhering to strict moral codes, White prejudice against them would disappear. At the same time, they were fully aware that Blacks were rejected by some Whites, primarily because of their racial identity, not because they did not measure up to certain social and economic standards.

Marie and Garfield Chambers

Garfield and Marie Chambers were moderates in their attitudes and relationships with Whites. These attitudes were always reflected in the principles by which they tried to raise their own children and grandchildren: that all people must learn to live together in this world and to tolerate each other. Their basic principle was to live and let live. The Chambers taught their children at an early age to work and to accept responsibility for their own welfare, as well as for the welfare of other members of the family. Although they were never prone to compare themselves to Whites economically, educationally, socially, or otherwise, they would always tell their children that they could be as good or bad, as successful or ineffectual, or as beautiful or homely as any other human being.

Garfield and Marie knew the value of voting in governmental elections. However, picketing, marching, and public demonstrations were neither activities they chose nor advocated to their children as events in which to participate. Blacks throughout the state of Texas, as a whole, did not engage in such activities. In order to remove racial barriers to their progress, the Chambers' philosophy favored self-improvement efforts, such as working through the church, buying their own land, strengthening family life, living according to the highest moral principles, and, most of all, getting a good education. As a child, I was greatly influenced by the Chambers' philosophy. Even as an adult today, I find that this same philosophy governs me and our family members of the later generations. ✠

Map 1.1. Ghana, West Africa, *circa* 1054 B.C.

Facts About Ghana

Ghana is a state located in West Africa and is near the Niger River and other important streams of water. Around 1054 B.C., it covered an area from fifty to sixty thousand square miles in what today are parts of Mauritania, Senegal, and Malia. Known as the "land of gold," Ghana became a mighty military power and lasted for over one thousand years for two reasons: (1) It controlled the greatest source of gold for Europe and Asia, and (2) iron mining and manufacturing were among its major commercial activities.

Occupations were mixed. The farmers grew wheat, cotton, corn, sorghum, and yams. They raised cows, goats, camel, and sheep. The iron industry, mining, and numerous crafts were organized as secret societies called guilds: blacksmiths, goldsmiths, weavers, cabinetmakers, and furniture makers. Ghana's kingdom eventually spread all the way to the Atlantic Ocean, but by 1054 B.C., the kingdom of Ghana was devastated by Muslim rulers who plundered their property and scattered the people. The authority of the kings of Ghana was destroyed, and the inhabitants were reduced to slavery.

My review of Basil Davidson's book *The Lost Cities of Africa* supports the fact that the African feudalistic system and African historiography have undergone many changes since the year 1054 B.C. Consequently, the map of Africa, shown above, has been amended to reflect such changes today.

Although uncertain, I believe it is quite possible that early ancestors of the Reese and the Chambers families may have been among the people who were captured and brought to Virginia and sold as servants. I shall continue to search for other facts to support my belief.

4

Map 1.2. Bastrop County General Highway Map

Basic to understanding the ecological patterns of the Reese and the Chambers families, we must be able to follow the geographical locations of the communities in Texas where they chose to live. Utilizing the above map, provided courtesy of the city of Bastrop, Texas Chamber of Commerce, and a copy of the Census Data, I am able to show geographically the locations of the home places and farmlands of the Reese and the Chambers families. This is where they grew up, sharecropped, owned property and land, and raised their families in the rural areas of Bastrop County and Wilbarger Community. The Chambers family would later move to the urban community of Austin, Texas.

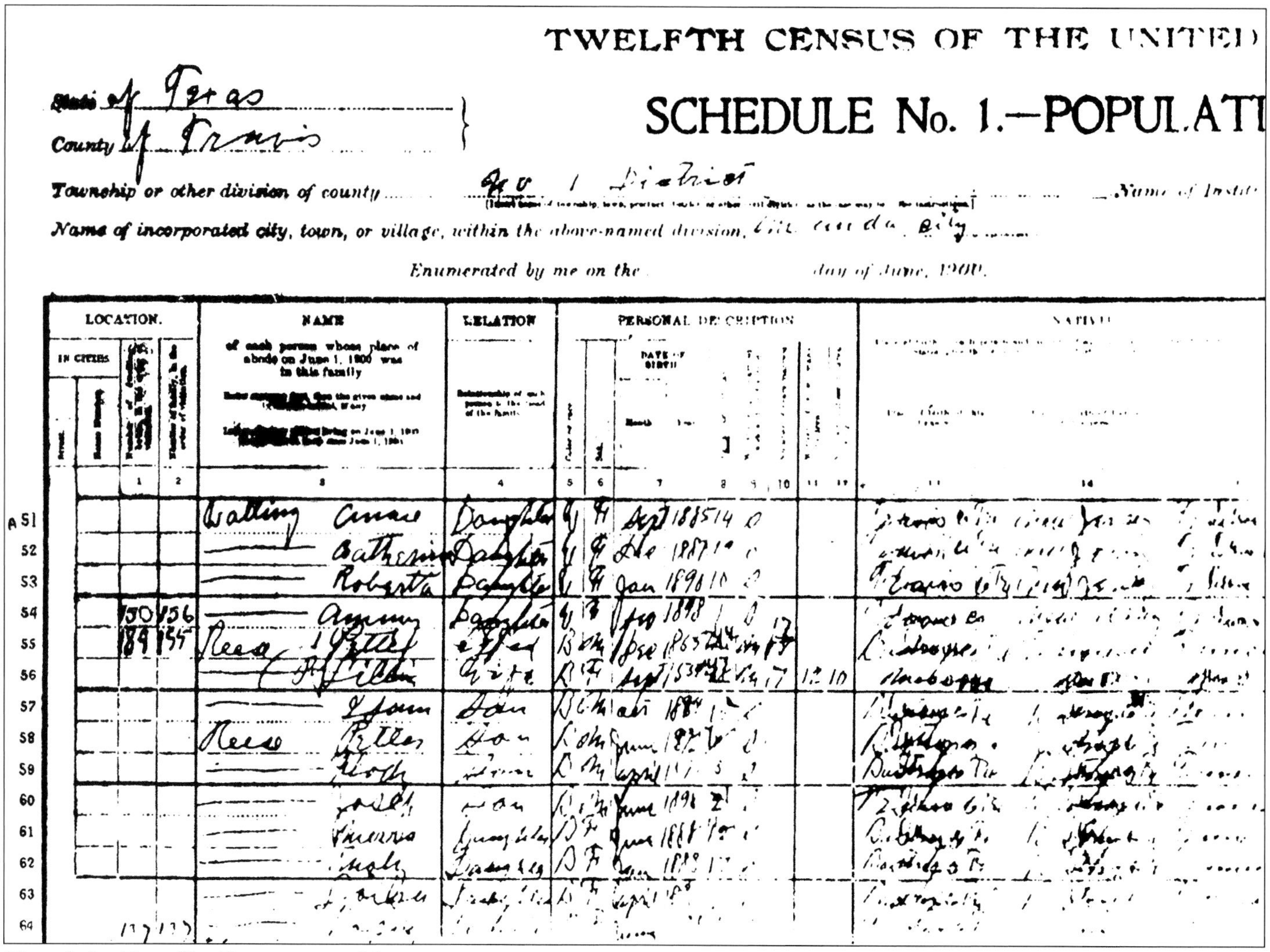

TWELFTH CENSUS OF THE UNITED

SCHEDULE No. 1.—POPULATI

State of Texas

County of Travis

Township or other division of county No. 1 District

Name of incorporated city, town, or village, within the above-named division,

Enumerated by me on the day of June, 1900.

Fig. 1.1. Family Demographics

Peter and Lilia Reese settled in the little community of Sayers (later called Sayersville) around 1865. Census records of the state of Texas, County of Travis, No. 1 District, confirm that fourteen children were born to this union.

Family Roots

(A Symbol of Growth)

Peter and Lilia Baltimore Reese settled in the little community of Sayersville, Texas, around 1865. Lilia gave birth to fourteen children, five boys and nine girls. As a family, they raised these children, farmed their own fifteen acres of land, and had some pasture for livestock. Although I never met Great-grandpa Peter, I do remember Great-grandma Lilia well. For a woman who was blind and 110 years of age, she was still quite active.

Like her mother, Marie Chambers gave birth to a large brood of children, twelve in all. The family moved to the Wilbarger farm in Bastrop County, where they farmed as share-croppers and began to develop their family treasures, of which we are all descendants.

The Chambers Family, 1925: (front row, left to right) Norris, Seallen, Baby Clifford, Thelma, and Mary; (second row) Ethel, Garfield, Henry, and Marie; (back row) James A., Leon, and Alberta.

Marie's daughter Ethel, my mother, became the single most influential woman in my life. Additionally, the eleven aunts and uncles were more like big brothers and sisters to me. I had a very special relationship with each and every one of them. Grandpa Chambers accompanied me to school on my very first day. The aunts and uncles loved us all very much. To the twelve, we proudly dedicate this book as a historic album directory for their families to cherish.

The Chambers family left the Wilbarger farm in 1935, moved to Manor, Texas, and, subsequently, to the community of St. John in 1939. By this time, most of their twelve children had grown up, married, and had begun to relocate to cities throughout Texas, the state of California, and elsewhere. Grandchildren extended the migration in later years to include Washington State, New Jersey, Florida, and Ohio.

Before we had realized it, we thirty-six first cousins had produced seventy-two second cousins, who have produced sixty-eight third cousins, and who have, today, added nine fourth cousins to the Chambers' family treasure. Sadly enough, many of our cousins, to this date, have never met, simply have never gotten to know each other, or have never learned about the Chambers treasure we share.

The Chambers Family, 1960

(Front row center): Mr. and Mrs. Garfield Chambers; (back row, left to right) Floyd, Henry, Leon, Ethel, Mary, Bernice, Alberta, Norris, and Thelma. Members absent are brothers Clifford and Seallen and sister James Ada.

Garfield and Marie Chambers

(Looking Back)

In recognition of Marie Chambers' one-hundredth birthday celebration on May 7, 1984, Ada Simond, a lifelong resident of Austin and author of a series of books on Austin's Black history, interviewed and featured Marie in her weekly article in *The Austin American Statesman* news column titled, "Looking Back." The author's account of the early years of the family life of Garfield and Marie Chambers was described so vividly that I was further encouraged to write this book.

In the article titled, "Farm Toil, Care of Family, Paint Rich Mural of 100 years," page 86, Ada Simond wrote the following:

Mr. and Mrs. Garfield Chambers reminiscing about their lives and family.

Marie Reese Chambers was born May 7, 1884, in Bastrop County, in the little community of Sayersville, to Lilia Baltimore and Peter Reese, a Baptist preacher. As a slave, Lilia had come from Missouri. Peter was born in Texas.

As a family, the Reeses and their 14 children farmed their own 50 acres and had some pasture for livestock. Marie Reese Chambers celebrated her 100th birthday on May 7, 1984.

As Marie Chambers looks back, she recalls that there was not much time for school. Her father did not believe strongly in education. There was so much work on the farm, and the family had to do it. Marie chopped and picked cotton, chopped corn, and did heavy farm work and fieldwork, as well as housework. They raised livestock for the market and for food, operated a molasses mill, had a vineyard, and gathered wild fruit. The farm included a good-sized orchard of peaches, plums, and apples for market.

The family smokehouse bulged all year. The deep well served as a cooler for butter, cream cheese, and other items. At the community cornmill, they ground their corn into grits and meal. The big black pot was used to make hominy and lye soap, render lard, and boil clothes. They made their own lye from ashes, which was also used as an insecticide in the garden.

The house was part log and part frame. Transportation was by horseback, buggy, or wagon, but mostly on foot. Neighbors were at least a mile away.

As a girl, Marie joined Sweet Home Baptist Church, which was founded by Rev. Columbus Collins in Sayersville.

Marie and members of the Reese family, however, grew up in the old Pleasant Hill Baptist Church, also located in Sayersville near their old home place. This church is currently pastored by Marie's nephew, Reverend McShan. Baptismals for the church were conducted in a section of Little Sandy River, located one block from the church.

At 19, Marie married Garfield Chambers in a big home wedding. To this union, twelve children were born. After the wedding, they moved to Bartlett, Texas, where Garfield worked at the oil mill and on the railroad, mostly on the tracks. From Bartlett, they returned to Bastrop County to the Wilbarger farm, where they farmed as sharecroppers. Their children worked on the farm when they were old enough and big enough. They milked cows, took care of chickens and turkeys, cooked meals, cleaned house, and did washing and ironing.

When asked what she was doing since the children did all the work, Marie Chambers said: "Having babies, teaching them how to work and be good people, supervising them."

Unlike Grandmother Marie's father, Garfield Chambers believed in education. Garfield enjoyed reading and encouraged the children to read. He found a way for the children to stay in school. The majority of the children completed the tenth grade, which was the highest grade some schools had. One child even earned a master's degree.

Garfield Chambers also made an honest living as a blacksmith making and selling tools, running a molasses mill, and was handy at carpentry. He even bought an automobile for his family.

The family left the Wilbarger farm in 1935 and went to Manor, Texas, and worked a farm for a share of what they grew. Life went on pretty much as it had before. They moved to the St. John community in Austin in 1939.

Marie and members of the Reese family grew up in Pleasant Hill Baptist Church, Sayersville, Texas.

Many baptismals were held at the beautiful Little Sandy River, Sayersville, Texas.

In her article about Marie Chambers, Simond further wrote:

Mrs. Chambers recalls that the Reverend A. K. Black was responsible for the family having a home. He sold them the land at a reasonable price and encouraged families to own their homes. The Reverend Black organized Blacks Memorial Baptist Church, where Mrs. Chambers was a member. She was the mother of the church by their choice. She prepared communion and was honored every Mother's Day.

Garfield and Marie Chambers were married for sixty-three years. He died in 1966, and she died in July 1987. They were the parents of twelve children, six daughters and six sons. Four of their sons served in World War II. All four received honorable discharges.

Marie Chambers' oldest brother, Isom Reese, lived to be 103. A sister, Lucy McShan, died at age 97. Daughters Mary Westbrook, 68, of San Francisco, and Ethel Hill, of Austin, have left their homes to live with their mother in this golden season so that she can remain in the home she loves so much, among the things that have meaning to her.

With her humor, Mrs. Chambers laughed as she said, "One hundred years, married 63, 12 children, one man, one father." Was she telling us something? ✖

Blacks Memorial Baptist Church

Marie Chambers honored at her 90th birthday

Don Chambers Jr.
Ragen High School
"Raiders"

The Chambers Family Album

Great-Grandsons of Marie and Garfield who excelled in athletics

Kevin Daniels
University of Texas
"Longhorns"

Odis Jones Jr.
Ragen High School
"Raiders"

Dudley Hill
St. Thomas Aquinas
High School
"Raiders"
University of South Florida
"Bulls"

Brothers Dudley Hill & James Hill II

James Hill II
St. Thomas Aquinas
High School
"Raiders"
Newberry College
"Indians"

The Chambers Family Fold

(The Twelve Chambers Siblings and Their Families)

I am indebted to many people for their assistance and ideas but to no one more than Cousin Helen Chambers Patterson. Early in my conceptual stage of developing this book, Helen convinced me that the ultimate purpose for undertaking such a project could not be fully accomplished without the use of extensive photographs of each individual and each family group. The personal prizes of everyone getting to know and to recognize the members of the entire Chambers Kingdom have lined the paths I have traveled for so long in writing this book.

Beauty, simplicity, diversity, and the great love we have for each other are what make the lives of the Chambers family so special. We often depend on one another for support, friendship, advice, tears, and laughter. Although each family member has his own unique views and personality, the family accepts each member as is in order to make the interpersonal relationships more enjoyable. As an institution, the Chambers family truly is a place where the members of the family make it special.

My first task in producing this enterprise was the recording of names and addresses by sibling family groupings. Photographs were collected from each of the twelve families. This has enabled us to track the various stages of growth and interests of both the children and the grandchildren.

With time comes change, and, we, as family members, have learned to accept and to acknowledge this change that affects us in every aspect of our daily lives. In recent years, our family has experienced many things that accompany a new decade. New changes among the Chambers family include an increase in the number of elderly relatives; family illnesses, which sometimes require changes in living arrangements; more students attending college through graduation; new careers and vocations; state and international travel; and more retirees among the first cousins. Although we often fear change, we must strive to remember the past and must push forward to the future to the new challenges that await us.

Photographs included in this Chambers Family Album will actually tell you who we are. We hope you will enjoy meeting us as we have enjoyed meeting each other through this colorful medium. Brief biographical sketches of each of the twelve Chambers siblings set the stage for a spectrum of diversity more colorful than a rainbow in the springtime. The offspring of the Marie and Garfield Chambers siblings reflects not only the physical and the biological characteristics of the family but also, in most cases, the social and the spiritual values as well.

Let me introduce Alberta, Leon, Henry, James Ada, Ethel, Mary, Norris, Thelma, Seallen, Clifford, Floyd, and Bernice.

Alberta Chambers Nash
Born October 30, 1906

Alberta Chambers Nash was the first of twelve children born to the union of Garfield (Big Poppa) and Marie Chambers (Big Momma). She favored her mother more than any of her sisters or brothers. Being the oldest, she had to assist her mother with housework and farm work while also helping to care for her younger brothers and sisters until they were old enough to share the responsibilities.

Alberta married Allie Nash. They had two daughters and four sons: Alfred, Herbert, Doris, Erma Jean, Melvin, and Leonard. Feeling that their two older sons, Alfred and Herbert, needed a vacation and the opportunity to visit and to work on a farm, Aunt Alberta and Uncle Allie sent them to visit and to help my dad on our farm in Manor, Texas, one summer. It took Alfred and Herbert only three days of plowing the field, pulling corn, and driving a tractor to learn that heavy farm work did not agree with them. My dad had to send them both back home immediately because they started playing around too much.

At her family home in Elgin, Texas, Aunt Alberta was known for growing a fine vegetable garden each year. As a young boy, I enjoyed visiting. I would pick blackberries and pluck apples, plums, and pears from the healthy trees. Uncle Allie owned and operated a grocery store located within walking distance of the house. He would always let me come over to the store to get anything I wanted: candy, gum, cheese, crackers, anything. He would occasionally let me ride in his big truck. I never quite knew why he gave me the pet name "Chinaman" when I was about five years old. I visited Uncle Allie the Summer of 1990. It had been almost forty years since I had last seen him, but he recognized me after about one minute's study and again called me by this same pet name. Uncle Allie passed away on November 7, 1991, at eighty-five years of age.

Perhaps the happiest moment of Alberta's adult life came the Summer of 1991 when her daughter Erma Jean moved back to Texas from Seattle, Washington, after thirty-five years of being away.

If you had traveled Highway 290 through Elgin on a warm, clear day, you probably would have noticed a beautiful lady sitting quietly on her front porch. That was our Aunt Alberta. After many years of ushering at Mt. Moriah Baptist Church, she quietly parted this life on March 19, 1997, at ninety-one years of age.

The Alberta Chambers Nash Family

Alberta and Allie Nash

Alberta at age 39

The Nash Children

Alfred

Herbert

Doris

Erma Jean

Melvin

Leonard

The Alfred Nash Family

Alfred and Octavia Nash

The Alfred Nash Children

The Gerald and Sylvia Nash Family

Gerald

Gerald and wife Sylvia with son Sterling

The Carla Nash Family

Carla

Carla's son Jeffery

The Reverend and Mrs. Herbert Nash

Daughter Belinda   *Herbert and first wife Mae*

Herbert and stepdaughter Natlyn

Belinda and husband, Marcus Harris

Natlyn and husband, Gary Barnett

Herbert and second wife Faye with grandson Philip, Natlyn and Gary Barnett's son.

The Doris Nash White Family

Doris and Claude White

The White Children

Donna and husband

Claude Jr.

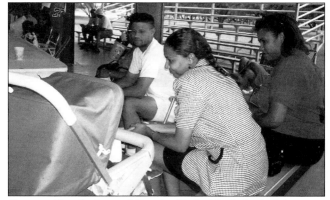

Donna, Claude Jr., and Cousin Cindy Machal admiring
Donna's son Jonovan at a family picnic.

The Donna Linton Family

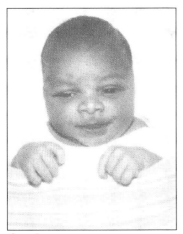

Son Jonovan

Son Joseph

The Claude Jr. & Carrie White Family

Hannah and Madison

The Erma Jean Nash George Family

Erma Jean

Daughter Cindy Machal

The Melvin Nash Family

Melvin and Gerri Nash

The Melvin Nash Children

Kathleen

Sons Charles McKiney and Andre Jackson

Herbert

Christopher

James Rivers and wife Dorothy with son Joseph and daughter Taylor

Christopher's son, Cole Allen

The Leonard Nash Family

Leonard and Elizabeth Nash

The Leonard Nash Children

Tony

La Shawn

Tony's son, Tony Tarrell

La Shawn's son, Tevin White

Leon Chambers
Born February 4, 1908

Leon Chambers was the first boy and the second oldest child. He was also the largest and the tallest of the twelve children, standing 6 feet 3 inches in stature and weighing 210 pounds. Big Poppa relied heavily upon Uncle Leon to assist with planting and harvesting the crops and doing whatever was necessary to support the family and operate the farm. Because of this strong reliance and responsibility, Leon's formal education was very limited. He also was exempt from military duties because of federal regulations.

Leon married Aunt Ida later in life. They moved into their own home, which was about five miles down the road from the family home. Leon became ill and underwent surgery several years after marrying. As a young boy, I remember walking miles each night with Big Momma to visit and to be with him while he was in the hospital in Elgin.

After moving from the farm, Leon and Ida bought a home in St. John, where he lived and worked for the Texas Highway Patrol for thirty years before retiring. One of the saddest occasions for me was taking Uncle Leon to the hospital when he became seriously ill in 1976. He, my mother Ethel, and I, selected grave sites for them and their spouses that same day. He passed away on April 9, 1977.

Leon was presented with a plaque by his supervisor on his retirement day from the Texas Highway Patrol after completing 30 years of service.

Leon Chambers was an honorable man, a deacon in his church, and was never too busy to enjoy spending time with his sisters and brothers, mom and dad, nieces and nephews. He had no children of his own. He was responsible for getting my mother to learn to drive a car and for passing the driver's test to get her operator's license, something none of us were ever able to do as children while still living at home.

As did many of my other relatives, Leon gave me the pet name of "Manboy" because I had learned to do so many things at a young age and because I stayed busy working around adults instead of playing with other kids. He often said that I would try almost anything and would learn it quickly. Approximately three years following his death, Ida became ill and had to be placed in a rest home, where she passed away on October 6, 1981.

Henry Chambers
Born May 7, 1911

Henry Chambers, the second oldest boy, was short in stature like his father Garfield. I am his shortest nephew! As the third oldest child, Henry shared the responsibility of running the farm with his father and Leon at an early age. According to his father's philosophy, it was the boys responsibility to perform all the family duties outside the house while the girls assisted their mother with the inside chores.

Henry became one of Austin's best-known masons. He built many rock and brick homes and other structures throughout Travis County. His former wives, Sedalia and Hattie, were schoolteachers, and his widow, Ida, was also an educator.

Uncle Henry's greatest hobby was fishing. He held the record for the largest catfish caught from the Colorado River (60 lbs) by a family member. Henry was also a great dancer and lover of music. He loved boats and boating activities, but almost everyone will agree that he was not the best captain of a boat. Although he had no children of his own, he and his wife devoted much time to their nieces and nephews, especially our youngest cousin, Dwight. Gathering his nieces and nephews around him for a picnic, an outing of fishing, or simply to listen to blues and pop music was his favorite pastime.

One day in 1944, while making some repairs under his automobile, the jack shifted, thereby pinning Henry underneath the car for almost fifteen minutes before being noticed by his wife and two neighbors, who ultimately came to his rescue. The front axle of the car had been resting on Henry's chest and collarbone for the whole time. So frightened by the scene of this accident, the three rescuers were given miraculous strength from God, sufficient to lift the car, and pulled Henry's body from underneath, thereby preventing a fatal accident.

Henry and Sedalia (his first wife, deceased).

Henry and his third wife, Ida

The former Mrs. Hattie Chambers.

Henry was a member of Greater Mount Zion Baptist Church, where he served as a deacon for many years until ill-health intervened. He departed this life on December 31, 2001, at the Walnut Hill Nursing Center at the age of ninety years.

A host of friends and relatives celebrated his homegoing at the memorial reception following the funeral service. Photographs of the audience are shown below.

Henry's Memorial Luncheon

The Clifford Chambers family members

Mary Westbrook and family with cousin Horace Lee

Ida Chambers (front left) with relatives and friends

Henry's great-nephews and great-niece

Relatives and friends

The Floyd Chambers family members

Henry's great-great nieces with father, Ralph Taylor

Eva Mosby and son-in-law Jim

James Ada Elizabeth Chambers Roberts
Born March 6, 1912

James Ada Elizabeth, second daughter and fourth oldest sibling, grew up in Bastrop County. She was always quite interested in education and cultural affairs. Aunt James particularly enjoyed reading and storytelling. She was fondest of horror and mystery stories. James Ada was very superstitious. Some of the stories she often shared at bedtime with our family would keep me awake all night. She actually did believe in the power of witchcraft and death spirits of the past that were capable of reappearing in the future.

After moving to Houston, Aunt James married the Reverend Benjamin H. Roberts. To this union, four children were born: Benzella, Bertrand, Myra, and John. Reverend Roberts was one of the most outstanding ministers of his time in Texas. He loved and cared for his children and family with the greatest devotion. Pulling his children to our outdoor toilet facility in my little red wagon while visiting us on the farm in Manor was not unusual for Uncle Roberts. The Roberts family has been the single most productive of all the Chambers brothers and sisters. To this day, a total of eighteen grandchildren and twenty-five great-grandchildren have been born to this family alone.

In spite of her tendency to scare some of her nieces and nephews with her dramatic ghost stories and accounts of evil spirits burying spoons and knives under the steps, Aunt James became increasingly popular among the teenagers of our family. A visit to the Roberts home in Houston was always a delightful experience, as she would prepare a big meal and sit down with us kids to discuss social issues, such as dating and courtship, letters of correspondence, poems and books. Aunt James was also an intense listener.

The attention Aunt James gave to others when they were talking made them aware of her interest in hearing what they had to say, including their views and opinions, which she respected to the fullest. With the passing away of Reverend Roberts on November 16, 1962, Aunt James devoted the remaining years of her life caring for her children and assisting them in the rearing of her grandchildren, whom she loved so dearly. James Ada passed away on November 9,1989.

The James Ada Chambers Roberts Family

James Ada and Rev. Benjamin Roberts

A family classic photo of James Ada, her older daughter, Benzella (left), and older son, Bertrand (right), 1942.

The Roberts Children

Benzella

Myra

Bertrand

John

Benzella and children

Son Paul and daughter Benzella

Granddaughter Lanora   Son Tessell   Daughter Lyndia

Great Grandson Shamarchs

Daughter Lyndia and son Tessel, with children

Daughter Mary

Granddaughter Maranda   Daughter Madeline

Daughters Mary, Madeline, and Mavis, with children

Daughter Venetta D. Mackey with husband David and daughter Jennifer.

Venetta's son Garric

Venetta's son David and daughter Jennifer.

Madeline's son Travis

The Bertrand Roberts Family

Bertrand H. and Doris Roberts (right side of photo) with children and grandchildren.

Daughter Rita Williams and husband

The Damita Roberts Family

Son Justin

Daughter Anitra with son Tyler.

Daughter Nakiesha

Nakiesha's son Patrik.

The Dionne Roberts Peters Family

Dionne (center rear), Son Michael (l), Son Aaron (r), Daughter Courtney (c).

Myra Roberts Fleeks

Son Roderick

Daughter Erica

Erica's daughter Paige

Erica's son Cameron

The John Roberts Family

John M. Roberts and Rebecca

The Roberts Children

Suzette

John Jr. with sisters Suzette and Bethel

Bethel

John Jr.'s daughter Rochelle.

John Jr.

John Jr.'s son and daughter John III and Courtney.

Ethel Chambers Hill
Born January 17, 1913

My mother, Ethel Chambers Hill, was the fifth child born to Garfield and Marie Chambers. She was the shortest of the six daughters, had a fair, reddish complexion, and shared many of her father's physical features. Her fiery personality won for her the distinction of being called Aunt "Red" by all of her nieces and nephews.

She married my father, William "Will" Hill, in 1932. My sister Minnie and I were born from that union. Mother divorced my father when I was about two and one-half years of age. Following their divorce, she married my stepfather, Eugene Hill (Mr. E.J.), and remained with him until he died on November 23, 1976. Will Hill subsequently passed away on April 23, 1989.

Ethel, 1980

Eugene Hill, my stepfather,
Ethel's second husband.

William Hill, my father,
Ethel's first husband.

The Ethel Hill Family

Son Jim, Daughter Minnie, and Ethel, 1946.

Minnie, 1991

Jim, 1998

Mother's entire adult life had always been centered around my sister Minnie and me. Even through some difficult years of divorce and remarriage, Mother, with the help of her mother and dad and sisters and brothers, always managed to keep our family together. She would never leave us alone.

Mother was the single most influential person in my life. Her strong sense of duty and uncompromising willingness to be of help to those in need were the most dominant forces in her life. I witnessed her seemingly forsake her own children to administer to the needs of others who were hurt or in want.

Christianity, education, and a positive attitude about work and the assumption of responsibility were principles she always tried to instill in my sister and me. Mother had always been the leader, by example. In spite of her need to work in order to help support our family, she always managed to spend some quality time with us alone, reading us stories, listening to us read our books, teaching us how to fish, gather berries and nuts, pick cotton, chop corn, milk cows, cook or clean house. She, along with our stepfather, enabled me to achieve goals I thought were impossible.

Having nursed and cared for Grandmother Marie until Grandmother could no longer live in her home, Mother returned to her own home and her old job of housekeeping for herself. If you were to drop by 7211 Providence Avenue, in Austin, you would probably have found Ethel sitting on her front porch or watching the *Oprah Winfrey* talk show. Whatever the activity may have been, Mother's heart and mind would always be fixed on Minnie and me and the Chambers family. She had lived alone in her home since 1987, but the condition of her mental and physical health was beginning to make living alone impossible.

On January 17, 1998, Ethel celebrated her eighty-fifth birthday. Although I was unable to attend the birthday party, I prepared for the celebration early by baking her a coconut-pecan cake for Christmas while spending the holidays with her. It was the first cake I had ever made.

The last year of the twentieth century, although sparked with several outstanding personal achievements, was possibly the saddest year of my entire life. That cool summer morning of July 29, 1999, I had to inform Mother of my decision to relocate her to a rest home and to board up the house we had built in 1942, our home for the past fifty-seven years. Victimized by Alzheimer's, drastically immobilized by two strokes, and thoroughly confused most days were critical signs that I finally had to make this decision after vacillating and pondering over it for three years.

Accompanied by her youngest sister, Bernice Toliver, and me, Ethel Chambers Hill was moved from her home and placed in the Monte Siesta Retirement Center on July 30, 1999, at 1:30 p.m. Only I am capable of understanding the impact her absence from all the significant events of my life and from the home she loved so dearly had on her the past several years. I could always feel her presence with me in spirit and hear her voice whispering wise words of advice just when I seemed to have needed them most.

On her good days, Mother had many wonderful memories of her family on which to reflect. She had memories of Minnie's family: her husband, Oliver Taylor, and their four children, Diane, Lester, Ralph, and Oliver Jr. She had memories of my family: my wife Eva, my daughter Eva Jr., and my sons James II and Dudley. Additionally, she had memories of my father's extended family and Mr. E.J.'s family.

The Minnie Hill Taylor Family

Minnie

Husband Oliver Taylor

The Taylor Children

Diane

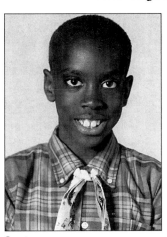

Lester

Ralph

Oliver Jr.

James

Eva

The Hill Children

Eva Jr.

James II

Dudley

Daughter Ann

Will Hill

Eliza Hill

Daughter Mary

The Will Hill Children: Ed and wife, Will Jr., Mary, Dan, and Tommie.

Will and his brother, Horace Hill

The Hill sisters, brothers, husbands and wives

The Will Hill Children Reunion, December 1984: (front row, l to r) Will Jr., Ann, Leonard; (middle row) Mary; (back row) Edward, Minnie, and James.

35

Daughter Jean Hill Freeman

Brother Jerome Hill

Freeman sisters with cousins

Niece Artelia M. Caldwell

Niece Irene H. Thompson

Mother was even more reflective about her grandchildren and their families. In Minnie's family, Diane has two daughters, Corbie and Tenya. Corbie has a daughter, Jasmin, and a son, Chester, making Diane a grandmother. Lester was married to Carol, and they have a daughter, Anya. Lester's second wife is Martha, and they have a daughter, Tamara, and a son, Brant. Ralph was married to Patricia, and they have a daughter, Raineisha. Ralph's second wife is Debra, and they have three daughters, Breanna, Linda, and Dyandra. Finally, Oliver Jr. has a son, Denerick.

The Diane Taylor Family

Diane

Daughter Corbie

Daughter Tenya

Corbie's daughter Jasmin

Corbie's son Chester

Corbie and Tenya

Lester with first wife, Carol

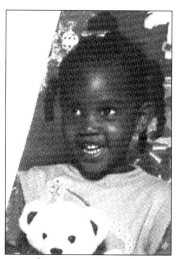

Daughter Anya

*Lester with daughter Tamara and second
wife, Martha.*

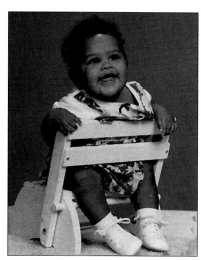

Daughter Tamara

*Lester with son Brant, daughter Tamara,
and Uncle Jim.*

The Ralph Taylor Family

Ralph with first wife, Patricia, and daughter Raineisha.

Ralph with second wife, Debra, and daughter Linda.

Daughters Breanna, Linda, and Dyandra

Raineisha

Ralph (c) with cousins Eva and Kayla Williams

The Oliver Taylor Jr. Family

Oliver Jr.

Son Denerick

In my immediate family, we had Eva Jr.'s marriage to Moses Taylor and the birth of their daughter, Bianca, little sister to Kayla Williams. Jim II married Ann Spulak, and they have one daughter, Faith. Dudley graduated from the University of South Florida in 1999 after an excellent athletic experience and is now employed with Boys and Girls Clubs of Tampa Bay, Florida.

The Eva Hill Jr. and Moses Taylor Family

Eva

Moses and Eva Taylor

Sisters Kayla and Bianca

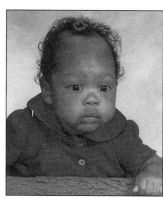

Bianca R. Taylor

Kayla Williams

Moses and Eva with his mother and sister, Joan Kiser (l) and Jennifer Taylor.

The bride and groom with members of the James O. Hill family.

Kayla with dad, Kenneth Williams, and grandmother, Bonnie Williams, at Disney World.

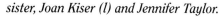

The James O. and Ann Hill Family

Dr. James O. Hill II

Jim proposing to Ann

Jim's prize snook fish catch of the day presented by Ann.

Dr. and Mrs. James O. Hill II

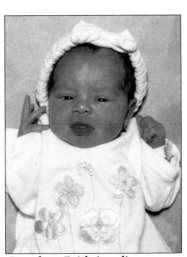

Daughter Faith Angelica

James and Ann

Ann accompanied by mother, Agnes Spulak.

Jim's trip down the aisle accompanied by Mom and Dad.

The wedding party, April 8, 2000

41

Dudley Joseph Hill

*Dudley "DJ" Hill, 1989-1990
Bernadette Elementary School
County Basketball Championship.*

*Fort Lauderdale Western Tigers Little League
Football, MVP Dudley, with Mom and Dad.*

*Dudley, St. Thomas Aquinas
School, 1993 Florida State Champs.*

*Samford University Bulldogs, Birmingham, Alabama:
Dudley #22.*

*University of South Florida
Commencement, December 12, 1999.*

*Dudley, NCAA Division II Senior All
American All Star Team 1998-99 at
University of South Florida.*

Minnie's death in 1993 was both a beginning and a culmination of her family's efforts to readjust to the unique circumstances faced by many American families today. The surviving adult sibling members of the family had to readjust to the absence of both their father and their mother or to the presence of a stepparent, who had to earn the trust and respect for fulfilling such roles. Garfield and Marie Chambers were keenly aware of such members in our family. Having recognized the critical needs and challenges associated with the roles of a nonbiological parent in a family, they seemed to have had a special appreciation and respect for those who displayed such characteristics within our family circle.

The extended or second family phenomenon so characteristic of our Hill family was therefore accepted with the highest regard and respect by each and every member. In such cases, the interfamily relationships seem to become closer and more intimate with the passing years.

Although Mother was rarely able to be with me to share some of the greatest moments of my life, such as my graduation from Howard University, separation from the United States Air Force, the launching of my career with the Boys Clubs of America, football games in high school, a reception party for being the first Black assistant city manager hired by the City of Fort Lauderdale, neither the births of our three children, nor the marriages of Eva and Jim II, I have always felt her presence in spirit. I consider my sister's and my accomplishments to be the result of Mother's daily prayers. In her honor, I present a written chronology, along with photographs, of some of the most memorable occasions to occur in my life and in the lives of my wife and children.

Ethel had only two children. However, Minnie and I helped to expand her family many times over, and Mother was so proud. With many fond memories of her two children, and without ever having met her two most recent born great-granddaughters, Bianca Rose Taylor and Faith Angelica Hill, Mother passed away on March 30, 2001.

Bianca Rose Taylor with Santa, December 2004

Faith Angelica Hill taking her first stroll, June 2004

San Francisco, California, City College, 1956

U.S. Air Force, 1958, completed basic training.

Graduation from Howard University, 1964.

Boys Clubs of America, Fort Lauderdale, Florida, 1968.

Administrative Assistant, Fort Lauderdale, Florida, October 1971.

Jim Hill, sharing his Exemplary Plaque with family members at City Hall. (back row, l to r) Moses Taylor, Eva Hill, Bernice Toliver, Ray Westbrook, Dudley Hill; (middle row) Kayla Williams, Mrs. Eva Hill; (front row) Jim Hill II and Jim Hill, April 20, 1999.

Dudley receives bachelor's degree from the University of South Florida, December 12, 1999.

Former Ann Spulak becomes bride, Mrs. James O. Hill II.

Members of the Spulak and Hill families taking photographs following the wedding ceremony, April 8, 2000.

Air Force father pins Captain Bars on Army son, Dr. James O. Hill II, May 28, 2000.

Eva congratulates son Jim, who received his doctorate degree, May 28, 2000.

President Ray Ferrero, Jr., congratulates medical school graduate Jim II at the Presidential Reception.

James O. Hill receives his master's degree from Nova Southeastern University, June 11, 2000.

Mr. and Mrs. Moses Taylor, married at Church by the Sea.

Mrs. Eva Hill Taylor displays her master's degree, June 11, 2000.

Ms. Joan Taylor joins Hill family

Honorary Doctor of Humanities Confirmation, April 1, 2001.

Diversification Celebration, July 2001; Fort Lauderdale Mayor Jim Naugle congratulates Jim Hill for 30 years of service to the City.

Growing up with our three babies has been adventurous, exciting, and fun.

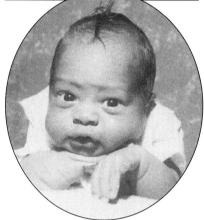

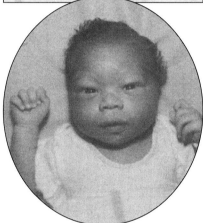

Baby Eva

Baby Dudley

Baby Jim

Greatest Moments for the James and Eva Hill Family

Miss Southern University Coronation Ceremony, 1987

*Little Jim's First Holy Communion,
May 11, 1978.*

Jim II, "The Butcher," St. Thomas Raiders;
and D.J., MVP Awarded 1988 and 1989,
Western Tigers.

Alligator caught by Little Jim in 1979, the Florida Everglades

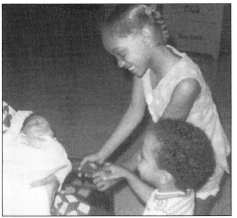

Little Eva and Jim II meet Dudley for their
first time on January 22, 1975.

James and Eva Mosby's (c) 50th Anniversary Celebration: A Family Reunion
for the James and Eva Mosby family, August 9, 1986.

Church visit with Grandmother Marie
Chambers (c), 1969: Ethel (l), Eva, and
Little Eva.

The James Hill family was featured in the Sun-Sentinel newspaper on November 15, 1987.

Commissioner Ed Kennedy dedicates Memorial Oak Tree in St. George Park for James Hill, June 1992.

FORT LAUDERDALE NEWS

LOCAL

Tuesday, Oct. 2, 1973   1B

James Hill City's First Black Appointed To A Top Position

Fort Lauderdale city commissioners today named the first black in the history of the city to a top ranking position.

James Hill, who has served as an administrative assistant for a year, was promoted to assistant city manager for operations.

At the same time, John Stunson, an administrative assistant, was promoted to assistant city manager for administration.

Hill replaces James Chandler who became deputy city manager of Hollywood six months ago.

Stunson replaces Robert Johnston who became city manager of Oakland Park six months ago.

48

Sunday, May 10, 1987 • Gazette Newspapers • Page 3A

Eva Hill wins Miss Southern University title

Almost every girl who goes to college dreams of being crowned Miss . . ., whatever the college or university is named. This dream became a reality for Miss Eva M. Hill on April 29 on the campus of Southern University in Baton Rouge, La., the largest predominantly Black university in the world.

Miss Hill, a junior at Southern majoring in advertising and marketing, is a resident of Fort Lauderdale, attended St. Bernadette Elementary School and graduated from St. Thomas Aquinas

High School in 1984.

She was one of four finalists competing for the Miss Southern University title. Her three opponents were each natives of state of Louisiana.

As a freshman at Southern, Miss Hill vied for the Miss Bayou Classic title and became runner-up. She performed in the 1984 Bayou Classic Football Pageant held in the Super Dome in New Orleans. As a sophomore, she was selected queen for Omega Psi Phi fraternity.

Winning the coveted Miss Southern University title means that Miss Hill will officially represent the university through public relations appearances throughout the country as well as become a benefactor of a number of important gifts and benefits to supplement her educational endeavors.

Eva called her parents — James O. and Eva Hill of Fort Lauderdale — at 7 p.m. on April 29 to report her victory. She took that opportunity to congratulate

her brother, Ji..... ...., a sophomore honor student at St. Thomas Aquinas High School, for having been selected by Clemson University to participate in a two-week seminar for selective high school students from throughout the United States this summer.

She also congratulated her baby brother, Dudley, a fifth grader at St. Bernadette's, for winning three first place ribbons in track for his school during this track season.

Eva M. Hill
Miss Southern University

Dudley J. Hill, senior student at the University of South Florida, Tampa Florida, has been selected to the NCAA Division II Senior All America College Allstar Team for 1998-99. This senior bowl game classic will be played on Jan. 30, at Florida International University stadium in Miami the day before Super Bowl 33. These outstanding college football players will be performing before coaches, and scouts from across America. For

some of the players it will mark the end of their football career, but for others an opportunity to perhaps play professional football.

Some athletes have enjoyed a history of being a key player and member of a Championship team in every sport they have played from little league up. Hill has been among this talented group. He has the credentials and

(Cont'd on 5A)

Dudley J. Hill: A Coach's Athlete

The Westside Gazette
Thursday, February 10, 1999

awards that have been constant reminders to him of what all it has taken for him to get there. Hill is a native of Fort Lauderdale, a product of the West Lauderdale football and track club, graduate of St. Bernadette Elementary and Saint Thomas Aquinas High School in 1994. A top athlete and student at both schools, Hill led both schools to winning their first County Basketball Championship and State Football Championship respectively in the schools history. According to George F. Smith, Head Coach of St. Thomas, Hill was the most committed, dedicated, hard working, competitive, loyal and respected athlete he has ever coached." He became the first recipient of the George F. Smith Family Coach's Award in 1994 for his achievements.

Mistakenly and inadvertently declared ineligible by the NCAA to participate in the opening game of this 1998 football season at USF, Hill quietly and calmly awaited for this crucial mistake to be corrected before the second game of the season. Coach Jim Leavitt, the team members and the Hill family were highly disappointed over such error, but remained objective.

It was on the Bull's first offensive play of the second half in the game against Valparaiso that Hill had finally got his first opportunity to officially compete in an NCAA College football game. Quarterback, Chad Barnhardt threw him a short pass which landed on Hill's shoe top. Hill caught the pass and advanced it eleven yards for a first down. His teammates and the fans went wild, but for his parents and the player it was one of the most emotional moments of their lives. Hill's dream of competing in a Collegiate football game had finally become a reality after four long years of waiting.

Hill's second opportunity to shine came in the fourth game of this season against Citidale. It was also the teams first time to play in the new Buccaneer Stadium. Starting this game as a member of the special team punting unit, Hill executed the only blocked punt of the game that set up a touchdown. This was also a big play for Hill who by the end of the season had spurred his team to an 8-3 record. Always the smallest in statue, but a giant in determination Hill has always reflected the spirit and art of being a team member and winner both on and off the field of play. "His ethic of hard work, positive attitude, and great efforts to be the best that he can be has served to inspire the whole Bull football team since joining the organization," said Leavitt.

Hill is majoring in Education at USF. He has visions of becoming a Physical Therapist and perhaps someday owning a partnership Medical Services Treatment Center with his brother, 2nd Lieutenant James O. Hill, II, currently a third year Medical Student at Nova Southeastern University. Both are the sons of James and Eva Hill, two committed public servants of this Community.

The Westside Gazette News proudly congratulated Hill for his outstanding accomplishments in football and for being a positive athlete role model for the youth of our community.

BROWARD METRO
Monday, September 7, 1987
MEETING THE POPE

Jimmy Hill: "I'll be a little nervous. It's only a couple million people watching you on national television — what's that?"

Everyone in Jimmy Hill's family is involved at St. George Catholic Church in Fort Lauderdale. He said it's their example that keeps him in church.

His brother, Dudley, 12, is an altar boy. Eva, his mother, is a member of St. Vincent de Paul Society, a Catholic charity organization. James, his father, is a lector. Now Jimmy, who's also an altar boy, has been selected to be one of 12 people who will carry offerings to the altar during the Mass.

"I'll be a little nervous. It's only a couple million people watching you on national television — what's that?" joked Jimmy, a football and basketball player at St. Thomas Aquinas High School in Fort Lauderdale.

Ethel Hill and daughter Minnie arriving at Fort Lauderdale Airport.

Minnie Hill visits Jim Hill Memorial Oak Tree at St. George Park, Fort Lauderdale.

Jim Hill and Mother Ethel in front of Jim's residence.

Granddaughter Eva and great-granddaughter Kayla, Magic Kingdom.

Ethel and her family at Disney World in 1993: (l to r) Eva, Minnie, Ethel, Jim, Kayla, and Little Eva.

Jim's night out with the girls: (l to r) Sister Minnie, Jim, daughter Eva, Mother Ethel, and wife Eva.

Dad congratulates son Dudley on his graduation from St. Thomas Aquinas High School.

Dudley and his best friend, Andy

Coach Conley and wife salute Dudley

Girlfriend Debbie hugs Dudley

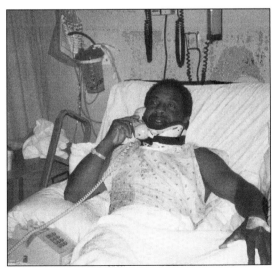

Jim recovers after spinal surgery

Jim returns home after hospital stay, 1994

Ethel had spent most of the first two months of 2001 between the hospital and the retirement center before quietly departing this life on March 30, 2001, in her room at the center. Photographs of her homecoming celebration reflect the love and respect everyone had for her.

Ethel's Homegoing Celebration

Jim supported by wife Eva and Mother Mosby

Ethel loved flowers

Reverends J.D. Cleveland, L. Patton, R.C. Smith

Ethel leaving her earthly home

Grandson Oliver Taylor sharing memories of Grandmother Ethel.

A family's final farewell

B. Toliver (sister), Dudley Hill (grandson), and L. Mackey Scales (niece).

Linda, Monte Siesta Retirement Center staff, with Ralph Taylor, grandson.

Neighbor, W. Alexander; son Jim Hill; Deacon Sweeney, Mt. Olive Baptist Church.

Nephew D. Hill

Mary Chambers Westbrook
Born June 22, 1914

Mary Chambers Westbrook was the fourth daughter and the sixth sibling. She married Ross Westbrook. To their union, two children were born: LaZelle and Raymond.

Aunt Mary and Uncle Ross relocated from Austin to San Francisco in the early 1940s around the pre-World War II era, where they lived, raised their family, and retired. Mary was the first and the only member of the Chambers family of twelve to reside, on a permanent basis, in a state other than our native state of Texas.

Ironically, Mary and my mother Ethel, who were born only eight months apart themselves, both gave birth to girls first and then to sons who were one year apart in age. Mary's children were raised together with Ethel's children, as though they were twins. They dressed Ray and me alike. LaZelle and Minnie also would dress alike. They took pictures of us, which, today, have become family classics.

Both sisters found it hard to separate from each other when Aunt Mary and family relocated to San Francisco. I remember the going-away dinner we had in the Westbrooks' backyard that evening, particularly the beautifully colored snake in the grass, which Ray and I spotted. At the time, we did not know that it was the deadly coil snake.

Jim and Ray, a classic photo of cousins.

Aunt Mary and Uncle Ross were both missed by all the family, but they always tried to keep in touch by spending their vacations in Austin each summer to provide an opportunity for us to be with Ray and LaZelle. We always looked forward to our cousins and aunt and uncle coming to Austin.

Always a true mother to me when I was living away from home, Aunt Mary counseled me and got me out of trouble whenever I made mistakes or used poor judgment. I always profited from her good advice. Mary and LaZelle always supported my sister Minnie and me whenever there was a need. Her son and daughter and Uncle Ross could always be depended upon to be there when I needed somebody. The miles of distance between us have never prevented the closeness we share. Who knows? Maybe someday we will all live together again in Texas or, perhaps, even in Florida.

As elementary-aged students, Ray and I learned a lot from each other. I would, for example, teach Ray the fundamentals of living as a country boy, going barefoot, making chewing gum from battery tar and gumalatch tree bark, or standing in the middle of an ant bed without getting stung. Occasionally, when Big Momma and Big Poppa were away, I would demonstrate for Ray how to ride their cow's back, much like Batman or Superman would do. Ray only watched with excitement as I would leap from the roof of the barn onto the cow's back, often falling on the ground and narrowly avoiding injury! Ray was always a good observer but never dared to learn any of these activities.

Ray is, and always has been, the best friend and the closest cousin I have in the world. I have always admired his great sense of caring about others and his spirit of giving and sharing. I really cannot say enough about him. We enjoyed being college buddies and growing up together. Ray tried to teach me how to be a city boy. He took me swimming at the city swimming pool in San Francisco as soon as I arrived there. He would encourage me to leave the house without a coat when the weather was warm because he knew I would freeze to death before returning to the house, only one hour later. His steaming open my letters from my girlfriends and answering them without my ever knowing truly amazed me. Our exciting trips to Los Angeles and to the Rose Bowl game in 1956 will never be forgotten. The Hollywood Flames dance and show we attended in Fresno, California, where all four of our car tires were stolen, will forever be a mystery. Our winning metals on the football and the basketball teams in college and basketball games in the car garage after school each evening seemed to make up for all the early years we missed living near each other.

To my dismay, Uncle Ross passed away on October 8, 1993. His son Ray continued to make annual visits to Fort Lauderdale, but the most important visit he ever made came on May 28, 2000, when I needed his presence like I never had before. Originally, five major events were to happen to members of our Hill family. However, because of some schedule conflicts beyond our control, we were given a reprieve on two of the events. So, on this day, at 10 a.m., James Hill II was commissioned as Captain in the United States Army. Just one hour later he received his Doctor of Osteopathic Medicine from Nova Southeastern University. The urgency of Ray's presence in Florida was to escort my daughter Eva down the aisle in case I was delayed from one of the two other events initially scheduled. The reprieve resolved that issue for the time being. Still, we all had to change clothes and be at Eva's wedding at 5 p.m.

Jim and Ray, escorting Eva down the aisle

The other two events took place on June 11, 2000, when Eva and I were awarded our respective master's degrees from Nova Southeastern University. Eva was awarded her master's degree in Education at 1 p.m., and I was awarded a Master's in Public Administration at 3 p.m. It was the timing of my graduation ceremony that was the concern if it had taken place on May 28 because the school is at the opposite end of the city from the church where Eva was being married. In any event, things did work out for the best.

Once again, as he had done so many times in the past, my Cousin Ray was there for me. My children call him "Uncle" because he has always been more like a brother to me. That dream that we had dreamed since childhood, to someday live closer to each other, came one step closer on June 19, 2000, when he told me that he had completed all formal requirements and was now a legal resident of Fort Lauderdale. We obviously had to celebrate! Big Momma and Big Poppa would not be surprised to know about our close bonding today. In fact, they both predicted it. The close bonding between our mothers, Ethel and Mary, had created a similar bonding between us. Good family relationships can do this.

The Mary Chambers Westbrook Family

Son Ray
Granddaughter Terri
Daughter LaZelle

Mary and Ross with family

Mary

The Westbrook Children

LaZelle

Raymond and wife Velma; cousins Terri and Eva at Ocean World, Summer 1970.

Eva and Jim's visit with Aunt Mary, Uncle Ross, and Terri, San Francisco, California, 1990.

Jim, Ross, Mary, and Ray in front of the Westbrook home.

Aunt Mary, Jim, LaZelle, Terri, and Uncle Ross at San Jose University Hospital.

Two proud fathers, Ray and James, with daughters, Terri and Little Eva, 1967.

Ray, Mary, and LaZelle, 1946

Norris Chambers
Born August 27, 1915

Norris Chambers, the third son, was an honored World War II Veteran who spent a number of his early adult years in the United States Army. As the middle son, Norris was always the center of attention. He was the extrovert, the most outgoing and jovial of all. He and his wife Elnora raised a family of four children, consisting of a daughter and three sons: Willie Norris Jr., Delores, Howard, and Paul. Willie Jr. is considered by most to be the best all-around athlete among our thirty-six cousins. Football and track were his major sports. Uncle Norris and Aunt Elnora always had lots of candy for all the cousins and relatives to enjoy. They built their home and raised their children on Providence Avenue, the same street where my home was located. Hunting and fishing were like a family tradition. Norris loved both, but he also found time to engage in many other forms of recreation.

Following an extended illness, Norris passed away on April 11, 1978. Elnora subsequently passed away on December 25, 2002. I feel honored to have been their nephew. Encouraged by his father and brother Leon, Norris became increasingly invaluable as a deacon at Blacks Memorial Baptist Church before his death.

Elnora

The Norris Chambers family, 1950: (l to r) front row: Delores and Paul; back row: Norris, Willie Norris Jr., Howard, and Elnora.

The Norris Chambers Family

The Norris Chambers Children

Son Willie Norris Jr., daughter Delores, sons Howard and Paul

The Willie Norris Jr. Chambers Family

Son Willie Norris Jr. and his son Corey

The Delores Chambers Jones Family

Husband Odis Jones and Delores

Son Odis Jr. and wife Shirrondra, their son Xavier and daughter Keiondra.

Daughter Lana with her daughter Alicia.

The first cousins: Xavier, Keiondra, and Alicia.

My unforgettable visit at the Norris Chambers home, December 24, 2002.

Willie Norris Jr. (c) embraces four cousins he grew up with in the St. John neighborhood: (l to r) Jean Yates, Jim Hill, Louise, and John Henry Fletcher.

The Howard Chambers Family

Son Keith, Howard and Carolyn, and son Dexter

The Paul Chambers Family

Anthony

Monica

Paul Jr.

Paul and Dorothy, son Anthony, daughter Monica, son Paul Jr., daughter Mary.

Mary holding niece, Keiondra Jones

Thelma Chambers Allen
Born May 27, 1918

Thelma, the fifth daughter, was distinguished by her outgoing personality and her vast knowledge of the personal lives of celebrities and Hollywood stars. She was very fond of all of her nieces and nephews and would often tease us about our childhood romances and other affairs. To me, Aunt Thelma was our family comedienne. She had the ability to make anyone laugh.

Thelma's great sense of humor and stimulating conversations made her the absolute center of attraction in her own household. Even before she reached the prime of her adulthood, she became stricken with arthritis, a condition which progressively limited her activities for a number of years before she passed away on October 13, 1980.

Thelma's spirit and love for her family became the source of inspiration for her husband Milton, Jean Evelyn, her only child, and all the members of the Chambers family who were fortunate to have known and to have been a part of her circle.

No greater love and friendship has a mother for a daughter than the relationship Thelma had with Jean Evelyn. The two were inseparable. Thelma, I believe, had always envisioned her daughter becoming a movie star or entertainer. Jean learned to sing and play the piano at a very early age. Her mother made sure of that. Thelma would have given anything to have been there to see her daughter give her hand in marriage and to develop into the talented, professional educator and woman she is today.

Thelma's daughter and "Shining Star," Jean.

60

The Thelma Chambers Allen Family

Milton and Thelma Allen

Daughter Jean Evelyn, the teacher

Jean and husband, Rutherford Yates

Seallen Chambers
Born March 17, 1921

Black is beautiful. Seallen, the fourth son, filled the bill. He was the darkest shade of all the members of the Chambers family, well-dressed, well-groomed, and multitalented. Although hesitant to go into the army when drafted in World War II, he served for a limited time before receiving an honorable medical discharge.

Following his discharge, Seallen wasted no time in preparing himself to become a licensed barber, as well as a licensed electrician. He was one of the first Blacks in Austin to receive such licenses. Seallen practiced these trades for many years, but he was always seeking to learn a new skill.

Seallen insisted that his sons' and nephews' hair be well-groomed. He often told me that a neat appearance and good behavior were essential elements for success. He would cut any of his relative's hair at any time, without cost, but we usually would give him twenty-five cents for the service.

He married his beautiful wife Lillian, and to their marriage, were born eight beautiful children: Charles, Henry, David, Don, Kaye, Joy, Kenneth, and Roger.

Several years following his divorce, Seallen was introduced by his brother Clifford to a lovely lady named Eunice. Seallen and Eunice married shortly thereafter. Eunice, a nurse by profession, was also a very active member of her church. Her active participation influenced Seallen to become an active participant himself. For example, I could never imagine my uncle ever becoming excited about modeling in a fashion showf. But he did! Eunice was very proud of this new interest he had in church life before his passing away on April 22, 1988. His whole family shared her enthusiasm.

I will always feel indebted to Uncle Seallen for the personal attention and care he gave me as a child growing up in high school who really wanted to become an independent person at that young stage of my life. He taught me the value of being well-groomed. Each morning before departing home for work, I would ask myself, "How well-groomed am I today?" or "Would Uncle Seallen approve of my appearance today?"

The Seallen Chambers Family

Seallen and first wife Lillian

Eunice Chambers, second wife.

The Seallen Chambers Children

Charles

Henry

David

Don

Kaye

Joy

Kenneth

Roger

The Henry A. Chambers Family

Henry A. and wife Beverly

Daughter Kimberly, with Beverly

Son Sean

The Kimberly Chambers Wiggins Family

Husband Vernell and Kimberly

Son Julian

Son Brandon

The Don Chambers Family

Don and wife Linda

Daughters Almuria and Bridgette

Son Don Jr.

64

The Kaye Chambers Bennett Family

Daughter Crystal   Daughter Noell   Kaye

The Joy Chambers Family

Daughter Jeanene   Son Lawrence   Joy

The Kenneth Chambers Family

Kenneth and wife Vann

Son Kenneth Jr.

Daughter Kennisha

Son James

The Roger Chambers Family

Roger and wife Vashti

Daughter Erica

Son Cataron

Son Roger Jr.

Clifford Chambers
Born September 9, 1923

Clifford was the fifth male sibling. I came to know him as conservative and refined, with a lot of human sensitivity. Uncle "Cliff" has won the respect and admiration of his family and friends because of these and other outstanding qualities he possesses.

He served in the United States Navy during World War II and spent years in Hawaii and the Philippine Islands. While serving in the navy, he developed an interest in food preparation, a skill and hobby which would later enable him to fulfill his role as both father and mother to his children.

I remember Uncle Cliff's visits home from the military when the family lived on the old Yancy Farm. He would occasionally join his brothers hunting wild game during his leisure or cutting firewood in the Post Oaks. On one such occasion, Clifford cut his foot with an ax and experienced extensive bleeding before he could be taken to the doctor in Elgin, which was about thirty miles away. I was frightened to see him in such pain and thought he might die. I was about five years old at the time.

Upon his discharge from the navy, Clifford came home to Austin. He bought a new Oldsmobile. As a third-grade student at Fiskville School, I was very impressed with his car and with his girlfriend, Rose Fennell, my Sunday schoolteacher, whom he married shortly thereafter. They roomed at our home for a brief time until their home was built.

Cliff and Rose had two children: Dwight and Nell. Aunt Rose passed away on June 27, 1983, leaving Uncle Cliff in the role of father and mother to his children. Uncle Cliff was the first person in St. John to own a television in 1950. My dad and I would visit him every Wednesday night to watch the fights from Madison Square Garden in New York. That was the first time I saw a television.

In recognition of his service and support of his family, Clifford was presented with an award at the Chambers Family Reunion held in July 1991. I was honored to have been a guest in his Austin home in early November 1999 while visiting Mother at the retirement facility. Clifford is an incredible individual and single father.

The Clifford Chambers Family

Clifford and Rose

The Clifford Chambers Children

Dwight

Nell

Rose (center) with Nell and Dwight

Floyd Chambers
Born September 4, 1925

Floyd Chambers was the eleventh child and the sixth son, the youngest of the six boys. He married Allene Clark. To this union, five children were born: Helen, Charles, Shirley, Samuel, and Michael.

Floyd was an entrepreneur. Business was always a major topic of discussion with him. He was an excellent manual arts student in high school. Professor James Mosby, my late father-in-law, was his woodshop teacher and taught Floyd to use carpentry tools well. Utilizing the skills he had learned, Floyd became a small general contractor and painter.

The summer before I started high school, Floyd opened an ice cream parlor on Chicon Street, which he called the Dairy Bar. He hired me on weekends to help operate the business. Floyd was a good teacher and in a very short time had confidence in my ability to run the shop alone when he had other business to attend to away from the store. Floyd also would let me drive his car to football practice and to Rosewood Park, where I learned to swim and socialized with my friends.

Floyd was like a big brother to me. I learned many things from him. When Floyd's own sons grew up and were big enough to follow him around, he always involved them in his jobs and taught them how to work, just as he had done with me.

Cousin Ray and I will never forget the exciting double date we broke with our girlfriends during our visit to Austin from college the Summer of 1956. Proud to have us home again, Uncles Leon and Floyd wanted to celebrate the occasion by taking the two of us on a fishing trip along the Colorado River one moonlit Friday night. So impressed that our oldest and youngest uncles were doing this especially for their two college nephews, we felt compelled to accept their invitation. However, breaking our dates with our girlfriends on that only Friday night we had to spend in Austin made us both sick. We fished that night for almost four hours and never got a bite. Our uncles were having fun just being together with the two of us. The only fun Ray and I had that night was throwing big stones into the water when our uncles had their backs turned and hearing Uncle Leon say, "Just listen to the big fish jumping out there tonight."

Floyd was very successful as a paint contractor, often getting more jobs than he could handle. The occupational hazards of painting were soon to have a negative impact on his health. He died on July 6, 1978, at the young age of fifty-three.

The Floyd Chambers Family

Floyd and Allene Chambers

The Floyd Chambers Children

Helen

Charles

Shirley

Sam and wife Tina

Michael

Sam and Helen, cousins Eva Hill Sr. and Jr., Shirley and Charles, 1967.

The Helen Chambers Patterson Family

Helen and husband Albert

Daughter Traci

Son Kedric

The Charles Chambers Family

The Michael Chambers Family

Charles and wife Joan

Son Warren

Daughter Sade and Michael

Sade

The Shirley Chambers Daniels Family

Shirley and husband Gerald

Son Kevin

Son Gerald Jr.

Son Samuel

The Kevin Daniels Family

Kevin and wife Tracy

Son Noah

The Samuel Daniels Family

Samuel

Daughter Jasmine

Daughter Paige

Bernice Chambers Toliver
Born August 22

Bernice, the youngest daughter and the youngest of the twelve Chambers children, was more like a sister to Minnie and me and to the rest of the cousins. We grew up on the Wilbarger farm together and attended the same one-room country school at Wilbarger, located within walking distance of the Chambers home. Bernice often baby-sat my sister and me for long hours on weekends while Grandmother and Grandfather went to town to shop or when they spent all day Sunday at church. To alleviate our fears about being in the big Chambers house alone when our grandparents were so late returning home from church, Bernice, Minnie, and I often spent our time doing fun activities outdoors until dark.

Bernice married Olen Toliver in a wedding ceremony held on the front porch of the Chambers home in St. John. To this union, two sons were born: Marshall and Ronald. Because Bernice and Olen were more like a big sister and brother to all of us, they somehow had a way of knowing about our activities. Their home was always open to me at any time, and their automobiles were always available as well. Both loved and collected music and could dance and play cards better than any of us. They attended all of our football games and always made sure that I was safe and that I had a ride home after returning from my late football road trips. They made so many unforgettable, kind sacrifices for me all of my life. How can I ever repay them?

Having lived in a rural community and having attended elementary school at Fiskville School from Grades K through 8, I learned about the many social stigmas of segregation and busing that first day I went to Anderson High School to start the ninth grade. Although Anderson was an all-Black school at the time, I learned how some urban Black students would often look down upon and make fun of us Blacks who were from the country and who had to ride the bus to school. This was most degrading to me socially and often made me feel ashamed. I tried to overcome this stigma by attempting to outperform my urban peers in every way I could. I was an honor student all four years at Anderson, president of my junior class, president of the student council, a member of the National Honor Society, and a letterman on the varsity football team. Bernice and Olen clearly understood the impact of these stigmas upon me better than anyone. Whether they ever realized it or not, they enabled me to successfully overcome these stigmas before I graduated from Anderson. They helped me to raise my head, to stand tall, and to achieve my dreams.

To this day, the Toliver home remains the central gathering place for all members of the Chambers family and their friends. Bernice's hospitality is as warm and genuine today as it was in the past. Since having to close down the old home place when my mother moved into the retirement center, Bernice's home has now become my living quarters whenever I am in Austin. She also looked after Mother on a weekly basis in my absence while also assisting her own family members. We subsequently lost Olen on October 2, 1986.

The Bernice Chambers Toliver Family

Bernice and Olen Toliver

Marshall and Joycelyn Toliver

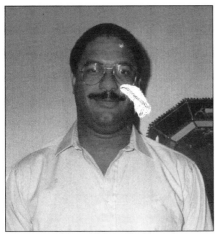

Son Ronald and his wife Cheryl

"Top Lady," Bernice Toliver, 1998

Bernice cruising in Fort Lauderdale, Florida, April 1999.

Nephew James and Aunt Bernice enjoying the pleasure of each other's company aboard Sea Escape Cruise.

Marshall and Joycelyn Toliver's Wedding, November 1990

Daughter Ericka

Son Trey

James Hill presents plaque to Bernice and Olen Toliver for hosting the first family reunion at their home in Austin, Texas, 1986.

Ericka's daughter Skye

Remembering Anderson High School Yellowjacket football stadium where Jim scored his first touchdown in 1955.

Husband Daryl, Erica, son Corey

Ronald and Cheryl's daughter, Erica

Son Corey

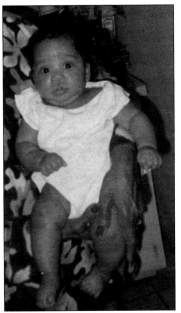

Daughter LaKayla

Cheryl and Ronnie congratulate daughter and son-in-law at their graduation from North Texas State University.

The Chambers Siblings and Their Spouses, 1961

(Front row left to right) Alberta, Ethel, Ida, James and Mary; (second row) Elnora, Leon; (third row) Norris, Ida; (fourth row) Bernice, Rose, Allean, Henry; (back row) Olen, Clifford, Seallen and son, Floyd, and Ben.

5

Down-Home Blues

(Remembering)

I had long wanted the opportunity to visit the old Chambers home and farm site located in Wilbarger Community about forty-five miles southeast of Austin. The Summer of 1989 afforded me this opportunity I had been stalking for over forty-five years. How did this all happen?

We had been experiencing one of those typical, dull hot summer days in Texas. The second week of the family vacation was rapidly coming to an end. Fatigued from completing a hard week's work doing home repairs for Mother, I called Aunt Bernice ("Sis") to suggest how thrilling it might be for her sisters and brothers to join me in taking a drive down to their old home place at Wilbarger. I had completely forgotten directions to the place, but everyone was quite sure that Uncle Clifford could lead us to the destination. We made plans to make the trip on Friday, July 27. Taking this trip was much like taking an exciting journey back in time to a destination almost forgotten.

Armed with my camera and accompanied by Mother; Aunt Mary; Aunt Bernice, our chauffeur; Uncle Clifford; and Uncle Henry, we boarded the van and were eagerly on our way. I sat in the back seat of the van at all times so I could be in the best position to observe the expressions and to hear the conversations of these five Chambers siblings who were making their first trip down home together since becoming adults. We exited Austin via the old familiar Webbersville Road. Once past the old Webbersville Baptist Church, the dirt roads and the farmlands we all used to know so well became increasingly obscure to most of us. The dust from the hot, dry soil became thicker, and the sand rocks and potholes in the road became larger and more plentiful as we drew near our destination. The rugged road was quite symbolic of the struggles and the hardships our family has gone through to get to where we are today.

The facial expressions and the conversations among the sisters and the brothers while en route to the homesite were most humorous. Ethel was all eyes, Henry was all smiles, while Mary remained in a state of virtual disbelief throughout the ride as though the forty-six years she had spent living in San Francisco away from her sisters and brothers were all somehow just a dream. Some of us felt confident that we could recognize certain old houses, fields, and creeks that we once knew, but Clifford was there to correct us diplomatically. Bernice could not do much more than keep the van headed down the center of the narrow, hilly, and winding roads. At last we had reached that deepest valley preceding the highest hill in Bastrop County. We recalled the steep hill we had all walked up so

Deepest valley and highest hill located in Wilbarger Community, Bastrop County.

Road leading to the old Chambers' home place: (left to right) Ethel, Mary, Henry, and Clifford touring the old Yancy Farm site.

many years ago to rest the mules that had pulled the wagon for so many miles. Furthermore, we also remembered that at the top of this high hill were the gateway and the path leading to the old Chambers home place and farm. The scenery overlooking that deep valley and hill was breathtaking to us all.

The anxiety had grown so within us that we had to stop the car for a few moments to catch our breaths, get out of the van, take pictures, and to allow our feet to feel the ground on which we used to walk, run, and play. Following our brief stop, we reentered the van hurriedly, headed down the deep valley, and up the steep, rolling hill. All of our minds and thoughts were focused upon the top of the hill with the expectation of seeing the old wood gate and path and maybe even the old home structure itself. However, time had erased them all. The wood gate had been replaced with a smaller iron gate, and weeds covered much of the path leading to the house, of which there was no trace. The old oak trees which surrounded the house were still standing. Just for the sake of reliving their old sweet memories, the sisters and the brothers grouped themselves together and began walking slowly toward the gate as if they were truly on their way back home. We were all charged with emotions. Bernice managed to hide her emotions by leaving the group to take pictures of the steep hill and the group of us at the gate. It was very hard to leave the gate because our minds had drifted so far into the past, and we felt that we had to enjoy these moments to the fullest extent possible.

Everyone returned to the van and claimed his seat. We then proceeded northward along the

Bernice Toliver photographing the old Chambers' homesite in Wilbarger Community.

Wilbarger Bridge and Creek where I went fishing with Big Momma and where Big Poppa, his sons, and I hunted.

old dusty Wilbarger farm road. Less than a half mile down the road was the location of the one-room schoolhouse where Mrs. Thorn taught Bernice, Minnie, and me. Time had erased the school building as well. There was a small creek and bridge not far down the road from the school site, which I had mistakenly identified as the famous old Wilbarger Bridge and Creek where I often went fishing as a kid with Big Momma and where Big Poppa and his sons hunted wild game during their leisure. Clifford immediately corrected me. Henry pointed out the field he and his brothers cut through on many nights returning home from visiting their girlfriends who lived about fifteen miles away.

We finally reached the real Wilbarger Bridge and Creek. It was as beautiful and exciting to me as it was when I was a little boy. I jumped out of the back of the van to take pictures while the others drove the van slowly over the bridge. I collected several sand rocks for souvenirs to bring home to Florida. Uncle Leon and Aunt Ida's old house was located just above the bridge, but it was no longer there. Once past Uncle Leon's old house, we knew that we were on our way to the nearest little city. As we were departing from this old Chambers community of Wilbarger, I watched the trees, the road, and the old houses through the rear window of the van until they disappeared from my view into the valley of dust.

Our ride, which had been so unbelievably exciting, was now taking its toll on us. Our thoughts were beginning to focus upon the little town of Elgin, located only five miles farther up the road. Historically, Elgin was the city where the Chambers would do their weekly shopping for food and items that they could not make or produce themselves. Elgin has always been well-known for its famous hot sausages, or "hot guts," as they were commonly called by us everyday folks. To cap off our historic journey down home, we rewarded ourselves by having dinner together at the old Elgin Hot Sausage Company, home of the original Elgin Hot Sausage since 1882 (Southside Market and Bar-B-Q), located in downtown. The dinner menu was simple here: hot sausage, crackers, onion, a sour pickle, and a big red soda pop <u>was it</u>. No plates, silverware, or glasses are required. One lifelong family tradition that will never change is that family members traveling through or visiting Elgin will always stop to eat some sausage and take a little for their families wherever located in the United States. If you happen to be traveling Highway 290 to or from Austin, stop by Elgin's famous sausage store or Meyers and get some. You might just meet one of our relatives there. These are the kinds of experiences that leave one with a feeling of those "Down-Home Blues." ✄

Chambers brothers and sisters enjoying lunch at the famous Elgin Hot Sausage Company

6

Peter and Lilia Reese

(Two Incredible Great-Grandparents)

Information about Peter Reese had been hard to obtain until the morning of May 4, 1997. It was revealed to me while having breakfast with Mary Westbrook in San Francisco. She was preparing to attend morning workshop services at the Zion Hill Baptist Church, pastored by the Reverend Sam Reese, her first cousin. A conversation arose between Mary and me about her grandfather. Mary informed me that Peter Reese was a preacher who had an excellent voice for singing. Sam Reese had many of his grandfather's physical features and other mannerisms. "In fact," Mary said, "when one is looking at Sam Reese, one can best visualize seeing Peter Reese."

R.J. Reese harvesting melons grown on his farmland.

I found it quite interesting to learn that Peter apparently did not like to perform hard labor such as was traditionally associated with living and working on a farm. He would always tend to shy away from plowing the fields or picking cotton, pulling corn, and cutting cane. His wife, my great-grandmother Lilia, would quite often be found performing these heavy tasks around their farm site. Peter enjoyed preaching and singing. He was also a barterer. Things he raised or manufactured himself were exchanged for goods and services he needed from others. He mined his own charcoal, harvested fruits, nuts, and vegetables, and took these items along with the butter his wife had made to sell in the city. Peter could always find ice to buy and kept it on his property when other people in his community could not. He would store blocks of ice in a wooden box underground where the ice would keep for several weeks. One might say that Peter was a preservationist because he had learned to preserve meat, vegetables, and many other perishable items from his earlier generation. Reuben James "Pie" Reese, (R.J.), my second cousin, currently farms land once farmed by his great-great-grandparents, Peter and Lilia.

A big, warm, and cordial smile is a Reese-Chambers family trademark which has been fashioned through all generations. Margaret Reese, daughter of R.J. Reese, exhibits this smile most radiantly.

Margaret Reese's smile is reminiscent of her great-great grandparents, Peter and Lilia.

Peter Reese was half Spanish and half Black. He had predominant Spanish features during his younger years, but his skin color turned darker in later years from smallpox, which he contracted in early middle age. His mother Miriah was Spanish, but she also had Cuban and Latin features. It should be noted, however, that, over the years, many Blacks have used these ethnic terms interchangeably in describing people having similar features.

Peter's wife Lilia was several years older than he. She admitted to some of her grandchildren that she did not like her mother-in-law Miriah when she and Peter first got married. Furthermore, she would not allow Peter to bring his mother into their house. Why? Lilia explained that, at that stage of her life, she did not like her mother-in-law because she was of

"Newlyweds." Center: Groom Lester Taylor and Hispanic Bride, Martha, accompanied by Lester's father and wife, Mr. and Mrs. Oliver Taylor (r) and brother Ralph Taylor and escort (l).

Cuban-Spanish descent. Lilia said that "rumors were out and around at the time that Spanish people were carriers of body lice. So whenever Peter would bring his mother by his own home for a brief visit, he would have to leave her in the wagon to watch his mules while he came inside. Considering the fact that so many of our family members are of Spanish descent, I found it incredible that Lilia could have had such feelings because, today, members of the Chambers and the Reese families have continued to select Latin or Spanish descendants as life mates.

We all were pleased to have learned in later years, however, that Great-grandmother Lilia confessed that she was wrong to have had such an attitude toward her mother-in-law and other people of Spanish culture. Lilia did not consider herself to be a Christian woman at that time. She enjoyed dancing and partying and considered herself to have been a woman of the world. However, when she became a Christian woman in later years, she changed her whole life and attitude about her mother-in-law and about people of Spanish descent. She had given her life to Christ.

Great-grandma Lilia's admission and apology for her stereotyping of Hispanics over a century ago served as motivation for me to meet and to get to know about the different people and cultures of the world and, in turn, to help them to know more about us. Meetings, conversations, and personal visits I had with the Honorable Reverend William Bantom, the Mayor of Capetown, South Africa; the Honorable Nana Akuoko, Minister of Culture, Ghana, West Africa; His Majesty King F.A. Ayi from Togo, West Africa; the Honorable Thomas Beltre, Mayor of La Romana, Dominican Republic; and Mr. Wang Xu, Secretary General, Hube Province, China, during the millennium year 2000 have opened the doors for achieving this important life mission.

From carefully studying relatives of our eight generations, we had learned that certain physical and social character traits identified in persons of the earlier generations have been manifested in the members of later generations. Peter Reese's love for his vocations of preaching and singing, for example, has been shared by relatives belonging to the fourth and fifth generations in the persons of Revs. Sam Reese, R.J. Reese, Clifton McShan, Herbert Nash, nephews and grandsons of Marie Chambers. Christianity and church have always played a major role in the lives of the Reese and the Chambers family members. This tradition continues today.

Great-grandma Lilia's love and talent for rhythm, dancing, and entertaining were as natural for her as preaching and singing were to her husband Peter. She often laughed and talked to her grandchildren about the effect fiddle and guitar music had on her. Every time she heard fiddle music being played, she instinctively would be the first gal to pop her fingers and jump out on the dance floor to cut a step or two. Her granddaughter, Thelma Chambers Allen; great-granddaughters, Jean Evelyn Yates and Helen Patterson; grandson, Henry Chambers; and great-grandson, Marshall Toliver; and great-great-great granddaughter, Bianca Taylor, all share these musical and dancing traits. Talking and entertaining people always have been enjoyable experiences for each of them.

Remembering everything that Aunt Mary had told me about Peter Reese earlier in the day, I arrived at the Zion Hill Baptist Church that morning with one purpose in mind: to get to know more about my great-grandfather through closer observations of Rev. Sam Reese, his fourth-generation nephew, whom I had met back in 1991. That morning Sam preached an inspiring sermon on the subject of "The Bread of Life." He also sang a special solo for me. He extended to Aunt Mary and me a most cordial welcome to his church, and his congregation responded equally. They could sense how proud

Rev. Sam Reese and Mary Westbrook, first cousins.

Sam was to have his own relatives visiting him. This was a very emotional moment for the three of us. We posed for photographs, embraced each other, and Mary and I boarded the "M" streetcar to return to her home.

Through his performance on this particular Sunday morning, Cousin Sam Reese, at seventy years of age, had enabled me to better visualize what Great-grandfather Peter Reese was really like. At times, I have to wonder if those cordial and emotional character traits exhibited in my day-to-day relationships with people are derived from the Reese side of the family. Although I do not consider either of these traits to be dominant forces in my personal makeup, it has been these two features that have helped sustain me during the most turbulent periods of my career in city government.

Intrigued by the insight Aunt Mary had given me regarding Great-grandfather Peter Reese, I continued to make further inquiries about Peter, his mother Miriah, and his wife Lilia through my second cousin, Otha McShan of Elgin. I contacted Otha by telephone on the evening of March 5, 1998, and discovered that he had firsthand knowledge about each of the subjects. He was most eager to share the information with me. From the sound of his voice, it was quite apparent to me that through our series of recent visits and conversations held during the past three years, Otha had learned to recognize me more readily than before.

Otha McShan remembers Grandfather Peter Reese well. He confirmed the fact that Peter's mother, Miriah, was of Spanish descent and that Peter's father was Afro-American. Although much darker in complexion than his mother, Peter's hair was soft, silky, and black. Based upon conversations Otha had with his Grandma Lilia, Peter Reese and she got married when Peter was about twenty years of age. Lilia was around thirty-five years of age. Several older relatives had told me that Lilia was older than Peter, but I never imagined her to be fifteen years his senior. Fantastic! I thought that there could be only one reasonable explanation for this union. Lilia preferred a younger gentleman, and Peter preferred the more mature woman. They loved each other.

According to Otha's recollection, Peter and Lilia owned forty-three acres of land located near Otha's parents' property just outside the city of Elgin, where they proceeded to raise their family. Peter died in March 1932, and his wife came to live with her daughter and son-in-law, Lucy and Elroy McShan, Otha's mother and father.

While living with the McShans, Lilia was approached by Leon Rivers and his son Steve with an offer to buy the forty-three-acre farm from her. Illiterate and not having the ability to write her own name, Lilia was believed to have been tricked by the buyer into signing her name with an "X" on an agreement to sell her property to the buyer for the price of only $93.00 for the entire forty-three-acre parcel of land. Lilia and the McShan family were not aware of the alleged sale of the property, even though it already had been recorded in the public records. Acting on Lilia's behalf, the McShans contested the sale of the property identified today as "The Hidden Oak Community," near Elgin, but the issue has gone unresolved to this date. The property remains undeveloped as well. "Little cousin" Otha remarked that there must have been a curse put on this particular property development because it has had nothing but problems ever since, even to this very day.

Because of the poor medical services available at that time, Lilia lost her sight in both eyes many years before her death. However, her strong mind and intellect enabled her to live a very active and involved life until 110 years of age. Many news articles have been written about Lilia in the *Austin Press*. I am honored to have been her great-grandson. ▨

Miriah Reese

(Courage of a Lightning Ghost)

Photographs estimated to have been taken a century and a half ago were my sole means of knowing exactly what the only known first- and second-generation members of our family looked like. These small photographs gave a glimpse of the earliest dawnings of the Reese side of the family. Believed to initially have been taken during the late 1880s, two small photographs of Miriah and Peter Reese were resurrected by Bernice Toliver and brought to Fort Lauderdale in 1996 to be photographically restored. No living relative of ours today, however, knows exactly when, where, or by whom the photos were taken, but, to most of our relatives, it really does not matter. Although badly faded, wrinkled, and cracked, they serve to remind us of the emptiness that our family would have experienced if they had not been resurrected. Without the photographs, our abilities to contrast and to determine certain biological and physical features of the Reese side of the puzzle would have been seriously impaired.

Bernice Toliver

Only a very few, if any, relatives living today ever recall having seen Great-great-grandmother Miriah during her lifetime. Mary Westbrook, Miriah's great-granddaughter, learned things about Miriah through conversations she had with her Grandmother Lilia. Based upon Mary's assessment of the conversations she had with Grandma Lilia, there appeared to have been very little social and family interaction between Miriah and her daughter-in-law Lilia. This assessment of Miriah, coupled with the insubstantial information that could be provided by other living members of the family, casts Great-great-grandmother Miriah's image as that of a ghost, a figment of the imagination. Why so? Because, almost as quick as a flash of light, Miriah raised her family and saw her son Peter grow up into manhood, get married to Lilia, and start his own family. Honoring her son's wife and respecting the privacy of their new home, I speculate that Miriah's time spent with her son and his family steadily diminished until her death. With her demise, the oldest-known

Mary Westbrook

generation of our family became extinct, and our shallow memories of her quickly faded into the past. Running through time, unaware that her great courage and hope would someday win for her the victory of achieving her goal, her quiet spirit remains steadfast among us as the "lightning ghost" of our past.

Utilizing her only photograph as a symbol to remind me of the kind of person I had envisioned Miriah to be, I often stare at her picture for minutes at a time without ever comprehending the essence of her soul or character. What was life like for her in the late 1700s and 1800s when she and her parents were alive? I thought about the fair color of her skin; her dark, thick hair; and her beautifully shaped lips. The whole issue about race and how her exposure to slavery might have influenced family members of today are thoughts that cloud my mind each time I see her face. Could Great-great-grandma Miriah possibly have a message hidden somewhere in her facial expressions that was never conveyed down through her seven generations of descendants who followed her? These questions still bother me.

In his book *Goodbye To Uncle Tom*, J. C. Furnas referred to a speech he had found in a 1955 almanac, attributed to "an Unknown." This speech miraculously answered these questions I had been pondering for so long.

I am the person who was born to live in a skin with a different color from yours.

I could not choose my parents, or you yours.

Thus, the color pigments imbedded by the unchangeable hands of nature in your skin are perchance white, while mine are black, or brown, or yellow.

But, underneath, I am just like you.

My muscles ripple in the same waves of power, and thrill to the same throb of joyous action.

My mind has the same function as yours.

I love and hate, hope and despair, rejoice and suffer, along with you.

When my children lose their chance of life, and become aware of the bitter road of prejudice that they must tread, then I know what my color has cost.

I offer you my hand in rebuilding an unjust world, that you and I can make better than we have found it.

I am the person in a different skin.

The intent throughout the above speech is both decent and constructive. There is a message about race and about the color of one's skin, diversity, respect for oneself and others. There is recognition of the fact that every human being is different, yet we share many virtues in common. We must therefore teach our children to respect people, not preconceived notions about them. Miriah Reese, although a victim of slavery, has become our immortal beacon of freedom.

8

Marie Reese Chambers

(From the Reese Perspective)

The general public, in Marie Chambers' day, supported by pronouncements from many leading psychologists and sociologists, believed that women, because of "natural instinct," were best suited to raise children and to supervise the related duties in the home. Women carried and bore them, so it was reasonable to assume that they possessed innate "mothering" talents. The ability to nurture children was not only believed to be a woman's God-given gift but also her duty as well. As illustrated earlier in this book, Marie Reese Chambers lived, and apparently subscribed to, this early type of philosophy about the woman's role in the family. Her reputation as an outstanding mother was easily recognized by everyone who came to know her.

Marie Chambers

Marie was extroverted, very sociable, fond of company, talkative, neighborly, and hospitable. The sociable nature of her personal makeup was best seen in the extraordinary preparations she would make to receive and to entertain her own family members, friends, and relatives. Holidays, Sundays, and summer vacations were her favorite times of the year to receive her guests. She spent weeks at a time baking cakes and pies of all flavors. Over a dozen live chickens and turkeys would be killed and plucked by her personally for the big feasts she would prepare for these occasions. Even though she grew hundreds of chickens and turkeys, no other member of her family was allowed to kill any of them except her. Violations of this policy resulted in punishment. I learned this the hard way by challenging her rule.

To get a more panoramic view of the personality of Marie "Reese" Chambers, however, I made it a point to try to learn more about her biological family, the Reeses. This included learning more about the interacting relationships between her and her parents and her sisters, brothers, nieces, and nephews. I have been fortunate to know these people, and in a few cases I have associated with them for a number of years.

My luckiest day in Texas must have been on July 15, 1993, because, on that day, I also obtained three other valuable photographs that I had been seeking for four years. Jean Yates and Marshall Toliver secured the most treasured pictures of Big Momma and Big Poppa, shown in Chapter 1.

Jean Yates and Marshall Toliver

To everyone who knew or remembered Marie, the word *family* was the subject she enjoyed the most during discussions. Big Momma believed that the primary purpose of the family was to raise children, to provide each person in the home with an opportunity for individual development, and to teach moral values by her own good examples. She would often say that "Respect for authority, to be obedient, and to honor and respect the rights of others" are the most important values for children to learn. She saw the family as being the most fundamental structure or group that all people require because this is where we learn to love, to come to work out our problems, and to develop our deeper feelings about each other. As a mother figure, she believed that for every member of the family, regardless of the level of kinship, her responsibility to them should always be the same: to love them, to be hospitable and sociable, to feed, teach, and to support them in every way possible.

About to complete my senior year in high school and to make plans for attending college, Big Momma summed it all up for me one day by saying, "James, you should always remember your family. You see, a strong family stands on the rock of stability and the warmth of the love they are willing to extend to each other." These qualities became her trademark among her relatives. They recognized and honored her by giving her the pet name "Babe."

Marie Chambers (r) with her sister Lucy (l)

Her brothers and sisters and nieces and nephews would often make Babe the focus of their conversations whenever they assembled. I vividly recall the very close relationship Marie had with her mother Lilia, who, after reaching her ninetieth birthday, would often come to stay with Marie for months at a time. Many times, their conversations were nonstop and would go on all day. Their discussions were filled with humor. Neither one of them had a good singing voice, but they could be heard humming old Negro spiritual hymns whenever they found themselves sitting or working alone. Marie helped nurture her mother to the ripe old age of 110 years, but she never dreamed of one day celebrating a 103d birthday of her own.

Sister Louisa Reese Adams and brother Sam Mitchell

Every time I pause to think about the exciting relationship my daughter Eva and I enjoy, I often wonder what kind of relationship Marie might have had with her father Peter. Unfortunately, I never remembered hearing her talk about her dad. Based upon information obtained from Marie's children, however, I learned that the father-daughter relationship that existed between Marie and Peter was quite ordinary for that time. Peter was regarded as the highest authority and head of the family. As a preacher, he placed great emphasis on religion and religious principles. Marie and her sisters and brothers all had specific tasks to perform around the house each day. Marie always respected her dad, and like all the other members of the Reese family she grew up and developed a sincere devotion to religion and to the Baptist Church.

Marie Reese Chambers was the first daughter of the children born to the marriage of Lilia and Peter Reese. Lilia, however, had given birth to two other children by her previous marriage. Marie therefore experienced growing up with half sisters and half brothers in the family, but she had a deep love for all of her sisters and brothers. She showed absolutely no partiality toward any one of them. They all reflected that same love and admiration toward her. Marie, furthermore, insisted that her own children, as well as her grandchildren, exhibit this same respect and love in their relationships with their stepparents and half brothers and half sisters. These examples my grandmother, Big Momma, had set made it so easy for me to accept and to respond to the outstanding fathering and leadership provided to me by my stepfather, Eugene Hill. From what I have been able to observe of our family clan today, stepparents and children, as well as half brothers and half sisters, are totally accepted and respected by everyone in the family. Marie Chambers could rightfully accept full credit for perpetuating this trend among all the families within our circle.

Marie was always very popular among her nieces and nephews. As a young boy, I was accustomed to living with and accompanying Big Momma on many visits with her relatives. I would often get jealous of the attention she always received from her young nieces and nephews. Becoming so excited in her conversations with these young people, Marie would sometimes seemingly forget that I was with her. I usually would show this jealousy by tugging at her dress tail or her arms. The nieces and the nephews always talked about how beautiful their Aunt Babe was. She enjoyed every moment of this glory and praise coming from the children of her sisters and brothers. As I grew up, I, too, began to recognize her beauty and the many outstanding qualities she brought to our family. Grandfather Garfield sure did know how to pick his mate!

While Marie's great popularity among her sisters and brothers was no secret to any of us, I learned through my private conversations with her that Big Momma shared a closer relationship with her brother Isom Reese, than with any of her other brothers and sisters. Their relationship was much like the one I shared with my own sister Minnie. Both were awesome conversationalists with a warm sense of humor. Always showing deep concern for each other's personal welfare and that of their families, they were cliques of the family.

Five generations appear in this photo: Marie Chambers (c), surrounded by great-great-great granddaughters Corbie and Tenya Franklin; granddaughter Minnie Hill Taylor; daughter Ethel Hill; and granddaughter Diane Taylor.

Through her interview with Isom Reese Sr. and his wife Viola, Peggy Trepagnier has provided further insight into the Reese family history by her vivid portrayal of their memories, family lifestyles, and the community where Isom and Marie Reese grew up and lived. According to Peggy's interview with both Mr. and Mrs. Reese, as recorded in Vol. 2 of the *Sayersville Historical Association's Bulletin*, Fall Issue 1982, pages 2 and 3:

The oldest person living in the Sayersville area is Isom Reese, a 97-year-old black man who, despite a badly crippled leg, has been a hard-working farmer for most of his life. For many years, Reese was a familiar sight along Texas Highway 95 driving his mule-drawn wagon into Elgin for groceries and other supplies. He no longer makes his trips into town because his eyesight has dimmed and the pain from his crippled leg has gotten worse. But his mind is alert and full of memories.

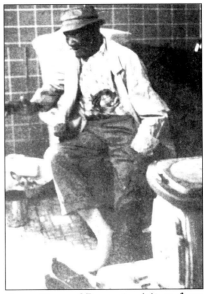

"I was born on the Henry Jones place, back over there on Spring Branch," says Reese, referring to an area which is now part of the Camp Swift Military Reservation. Reese and his wife Viola believe that his correct birth date is September 15, 1885, although some family members claim that he is older, possibly over 100. When Reese was a child, his family moved onto land northwest of Sayersville. "Over there where they got (those) oil wells, Papa bought a little place, right at 50 acres," recalls Reese. "And everybody (would go) together at lunchtime and put up log houses and take clay and lime and make mortar. . . . Old man Jim Perkins, Mama's stepdaddy, came down and put us up a brick chimney. And we moved over there. Papa said, 'I'm going to clear up this land . . . and you won't know these woods.' Which he did."

Isom Reese, 97, greets visitors from his favorite chair by the wood heater in his home near Sayersville.

Reese says his father dug a shallow hole for water. "Papa said, 'I'm going to stop the children from packing water from Little Sandy (Creek) down yonder.'" According to Reese, the family had plenty of water from the hole, which was evidently a spring.

During the time the family lived on this land, Isom's younger sister Maria was born, an event which Reese remembers well. After the birth "the granny woman" called the children into the cabin to look at their new sister. She told them that the baby had been found in a hollow stump, then sent the children back outside to play. "Sam Mitchell (Reese's half-brother) says, 'I know where that hollow stump is. . . . I'm going to go out and split that stump open and see if we can find one (a baby) like she is,'" recalls Reese. The children searched in two hollow stumps before concluding that the woman had told them "a damn lie."

The family lost the 50 acres when Reese's father failed to pay the taxes on it. Reese doesn't remember exactly how long they lived there, but "we lived there a long time, because we cleared up a big field . . . we worked it with two steers and an old mule." From there the family moved to Manor. Reese's leg was broken when he fell out of a tree as a child. He remembers lying outside on a quilt for four days and nights after the accident. Although he received treatment from a country doctor in the Camp Swift area, a Dr. Holt, the leg never healed properly and was badly twisted. "I walked on tiptoes on that leg and wore out the toes on my shoes. But still I worked." When he was older, doctors at Temple Hospital operated on the leg and partially corrected the deformity.

As a young man Reese worked at the Butler and Lasher brick plants and for the railroad, besides farming. The Lasher brick works was located near the railroad about three miles north of Sayersville. In 1909 Reese married Viola Evans, who lived in Sayersville. She moved to Sayersville with her family when she was 10 years old. Mrs. Reese remembers Sayersville as a thriving community with several grocery stores, a butcher shop, cafe, post office, and train depot. She says the stores, operated at various times by Nish Green, Iverson Clark, Calloway Barton, Charley Duncan, and Joe Owen (Bell's Store), sold mostly groceries. Another major business in Sayersville was the blacksmith shop operated for many years by Walter Madison. "Edmund Brice – they called him Bishop – operated a cafe," recalls Mrs. Reese, "and Sylvester Steward butchered cattle and sold beef. Henry Jones' son Charlie Jones was Postmaster," says Mrs. Reese, "and then we had Virge Clark, Iverson Clark's boy, and Carl Clark – I know those two because they tried to court me and I wouldn't have anything to do with them."

Mrs. Reese attended a country school near Sayersville. "Davis Byrd, Moot Byrd's daddy, was my teacher," she said. "He would tap every one of our lunches at recess – if there were a hundred of us, he'd tap them all – and when dinner time came, he was full." She did not attend the school which was located in Sayersville itself, but remembers when it was being built by Steve Price and his son Samson. "I was grown then and carried them their dinner," she says. She remembers in particular the big bay window they were building at the schoolhouse.

The railroad was a big part of life in Sayersville. Mrs. Reese remembers as a child laying pennies on the track for the trains to run over and flatten. "We'd sit on the depot with our legs hanging down and watch the freight trains passing by." When she was older she helped Wash Evans' wife at the section house washing dishes and setting tables. She remembers one railroad worker being fired by Wash Evans, the section foreman, for eating 15 biscuits at one meal. "A man named Brown pumped water for the trains, and another man also named Brown ran the section house at one time," recalls Mrs. Reese. "A man

88

named McDow was also a section foreman. Many area residents came into Sayersville to catch the train," says Mrs. Reese. "You could get on the local for 25 cents and ride to Elgin."

"Sideshows and con artists came frequently to the area," recalls Mrs. Reese. She remembers hearing how angry grocery store proprietor Iverson Clark became after an incident in Elgin. Clark had a $20 bill changed at a sideshow and later discovered he only had a pocketful of string. He went back to the show to complain, but that man had gone to Houston. "It used to be tough," says Mrs. Reese. "Some folks were so mean. Like Papa said, 'they'd put a spider or something in your dumplings!'"

Today Mr. and Mrs. Reese live on a small farm north of Sayersville. Although their large modern house is full of conveniences, such as a freezer and refrigerator, it is evident that the Reeses still prefer many of the old ways. Viola Reese still cooks three meals a day on her wood cook stove and prefers to do her laundry in a cast-iron washpot outdoors. A large wood heater provides most of their heat during the winter. There are two garden plots behind the house. "His and hers," according to a granddaughter.

At a recent family reunion, all of the couple's 13 children were present, along with 74 grandchildren, 64 great-grandchildren, 37 great-great-grandchildren, and 25 great-great-great grandchildren. "The Lord has been good to us," says Viola Reese.

After reading Peggy's story about Uncle Isom and Aunt Viola, my knowledge of the Reese side of the family had grown immensely. Actually visiting the homesite and participating in the Annual Reese Family Reunion have created a closeness between the Reese and the Chambers families and me that we never dreamed possible. The fact that Marie and her brother Isom both had raised large families of their own and always enjoyed sharing their family stories with others had become the basis of that close relationship between them that continued throughout the century of their lifetime.

I conclude this chapter by sharing with our family and readers Marie Reese Chambers' obituary, as well as treasured photographs of members of her own beloved Reese family from whom she received so much of the inspiration that helped her reach the woman of stature and strength she ultimately achieved. I recognize the fact that within Black American families today, there are countless "Big Momma" figures to be found. However, Marie Reese Chambers, Babe, Big Momma, is the one our family knew best. 🐾

Marie Chambers photographed in 1976 with her grandchildren

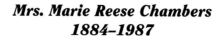

Mrs. Marie Reese Chambers
1884–1987

Marie Chambers, the second child of Peter and Lilia Reese, was born May 7, 1884, in Bastrop County, Texas. At an early age she accepted Christ at Sweet Home Baptist Church at Sayersville, Texas.

Later, she moved to the Union Lee community and joined the Union Lee Baptist Church where she served as an active member for a number of years.

In 1941, she moved to Austin, Texas, where she united with a branch of Rising Star Baptist Church which later became Blacks Memorial. She loved her church. She served as a deaconess and worked faithfully with the senior mission until she became disabled. After becoming disabled, she would still ask about the church and its welfare.

She was united in marriage with Garfield Chambers, who preceded her in death. To this union, twelve children were born. Four preceded her in death: Leon, Norris, Floyd, and Thelma Allen. Seallen, James, Ada Roberts, Alberta Nash, Ethel Hill, and Henry Chambers succeeded her.

Her survivors include two daughters, Mary Westbrook, San Francisco, California, and Bernice Toliver, Austin, Texas; one son, Clifford Chambers of Austin, Texas; 33 grandchildren; 69 great-grandchildren; 68 great-great-grandchildren; and 5 great-great-great-grandchildren; daughters-in-law; sons-in-law; nieces, nephews, and a host of relatives and friends.

Families From the Reese Generations

The Elroy and Lucy McShan Family

1st Row (l to r) Milia Goins, Gladys Barnes (Otha's daughter), Elroy McShan, Evelyn Flowers, Mary McDonald, Marie McShan (Otha's wife), Sean Flowers (Evelyn's grandson). 2nd Row (r to l) Thaddeus McDonald, O. L. Flowers (Evelyn's husband). Back Row (l to r) Otha McShan, Shifton McShan.

(l to r) Willie and Marjorie Clayton, Mary and Thaddeus McDonald.

The Mary Lou Benford Family

Front Row (l to r) Dorothy Heard, Andrew Benford, Leland Arthur holding Marquis Jones, Tyler Wright, Kendra Wright, Cierra Arthur, Andrew A. Benford, Britany Jones, Patrick and Trish Jones. Second Row (l to r) Mary L. Benford, Crystal Arthur, Carol Moses, Genevive McGruder, Cathy Moses, and Chanika Moses. Back Row (l to r) Mike Jones, Eric Heard, Marvin Heard, and John Benford.

Serving and eating with pleasure are Dorothy Heard and Genevive McGruder.

Robbie Evans Frazier's grandchildren

Enjoying the moments: (front) Ethel Hill, (back) Patrick and Trisha Jones, Jim Hill, Thaddeus and Lucy McDonald.

The Isom and Viola Reese Family

Sammy Reese, 1994 hayride

Robbie Lee Evans Frazier (center)

(l to r) Mr. & Mrs. S. T. Thomas, S. T. Flowers, Ivory (Teena) Flowers, Barbara Thomas, Debra Thomas holding Sterling, Gloria Murray with Jonathan Murray (front), Monty Jo Thomas, Ivory Thomas.

Rev. R.J. Reese

Ida Mae Edmundson

Mr. and Mrs. Isom and Viola Reese (Marie Chambers' brother and sister-in-law). Gestures help tell the story when Isom and Viola Reese recall Sayersville's past. They were married for 73 years.

9

Big Momma

(The Reese Reflections)

The older I became and the more I learned about Big Momma, the more I wanted to know that much more about her. There was only one way I knew how to fulfill this desire. I had to try to get to know the Reese family members better. Somehow, I had to get to know Big Momma's living sisters and brothers, nieces and nephews, and others. It was never enough to know them only by face or by name or by hearsay; I needed to know them as family. How they grew up, their occupations, religious beliefs, hobbies, talents, and their aspirations in life were all questions I needed to have answered. I felt that they also wanted to know the same things about us, the Chambers side of the puzzle. Motivated by this quest for knowledge, I could wait no longer. I took some action.

Rev. R.J. Reese

Ironically, of the living Reese family, R.J. Reese was the one whose name was most often spoken of by my mother and by my aunts and uncles around Austin. He was frequently described as being a most friendly, talented, and outgoing person who loved and thought so much of the whole family all the time. Having heard of this same description of him by so many people for so long, I began to focus on R.J. and could somehow observe a few of my own qualities in him. For example, we are both among the shortest males in our respective sides of the families, we share part of a common name, "James," we like growing things, singing, church, and we both have worked hard all of our lives. We are both proud of our families and are proud to be who we are.

Several years ago, when I first met R.J. and his family while spending my summer vacation in Austin, he extended a special invitation to my family and me to attend the Annual Reese Reunion and the formal opening dedication of his newly built church, Judea Missionary Baptist Church, located in Granger, that following Sunday. I accepted both invitations with great pleasure.

The Annual Reese Family Reunion is one of the largest annual events to be held in Sayersville each year, near the Little Sandy River. They have been having these gatherings for the past forty-five years or more. While attending my first Reese Reunion in 1991, R.J. introduced me to the Reverend Sam Reese, his older brother. Sam and I discovered that he and I had both lived in San Francisco. Historically, Sam has preached at the family reunion service held the Sunday morning following the Saturday picnic each year. It was on this occasion that I first met Isom and Viola Reese, the parents of R.J. and Sam. Isom Reese was Big Momma's last living brother. My visit to the Pleasant Hill Baptist Church that had been built in 1897 made me realize and understand how deeply rooted in the church and in their faith the Reese family has always been. Through their many years of preaching, ministering, and singing with such well-known professional groups as the Silvertones and the

Iowa Reese

Paramount Gospel Singers, Sam and R.J. Reese were only fulfilling the life roles their family background had prepared them to play.

Visits to the Reese reunions since 1991, coupled with the assistance Iowa Reese, R.J.'s wife, had given, enabled me to compile a relatively comprehensive collection of photographs of the Reese family. I reviewed each photograph intensely, but I found it quite difficult to associate names and faces of all the Reese cousins I kept meeting each year. I therefore requested that Iowa provide me with the names of each person in the photographs. Cousin Margaret "Cookie" Reese, Iowa's youngest daughter, spent many hours collecting everyone's names.

On October 21, 1996, I received all the names for which I had been awaiting so eagerly. Cookie had also sent me a most beautiful letter. Her letter illustrates and expresses, better than anything I have seen, read, or heard, the love we have in our families for each other and our yearnings to get to know each other better real soon. Before closing this chapter, I am proud to share Cookie's letter with you. Our grandparents, Marie and Garfield Chambers, and Grandpa and Grandma Reese would be so happy to know how our younger generations still idolize them. 🙢

Margaret Reese, her husband and two children

October 21, 1996

Dear Cousin James:

Thank you for being patient with me. I have taken on too many projects but am slowly narrowing them down. Well, here are the pictures. I am sorry it took so long.

Everybody is doing fine. Daddy and his sister Faye drove to San Francisco to visit sister Omega and brothers Isom Jr., Sam, and Earl. Most of their time was spent fishing, picking peas and greens, and hunting. Imagine driving all the way to California to do the same things they do here. Life is fair and full of much the same.

Let's see. Daddy still farms every day. Mama is taking a computer class. Kaye (my sister) stays busy with her children. Sam and Don (my brothers) are both doing fine. The weather here has been great – it's starting to get cool.

I would like to get to know you better. I know that you work in city government in Florida. Do you have children? What are your interests? What do you do for fun? What are some of the interests you face in your community? Have you ever thought to move back to Texas? How did you get to Florida anyway? Do you have siblings? When did you first meet my dad? Do you know much of our history? I always thought the names Isom and Marie were unique. I do hope that the stories in the book will enlighten me. I look forward to talking to you. I don't feel that I know much about the Chambers family. I am anxious to learn more.

There are certain qualities that are unique to our families – family devotion, hard work, honesty, loyalty, strong, kind, loving, God-fearing, and forgiving. I am so proud to be a Reese. I could never understand how Grandpa Reese and Grandma Reese could have so many children and grandchildren, etc., etc., and never favor one over the other. We each thought we were the favorite one. That's a wonderful thought . . . We were all the favorite one. It wasn't until I understood God's love for (us) and that he died for me. Some of my most favorite thoughts are those remembering my grandparents. Papa always had such a joking demeanor and Grandma had excellent recall for such things as when Mr. Joe died or when Miss Jane got married. Sitting around the wood-burning stove while Papa told stories while Grandma sang Zion hymns and cooked biscuits – those were the days. Thanks for capturing this piece of our history so that I and my children will not forget.

It's late. I'll talk to you later. Love ya.

Your Cousin,

Cookie

10

The Garfield Chambers Family

(The Tragedy of Great-Great-Grandfather Henry Chambers)

Garfield Chambers

Excavating the Chambers Family Treasure had covered a span of over sixteen years. I had utilized every means possible to get to know, for myself, firsthand, each member of the Chambers clan. The individual discussions and visits I had with family members whom I had never known created a greater urge within me to search deeper into this family's history. Although money was scarce for me at times, I never hesitated to catch an airplane, rent a car, place a long-distance telephone call, or drive my car all night long to find answers to the many questions I had asked about our family. I have committed the rest of my life to this search and hope that someone in my family will continue the search when I am gone.

Like many Black American families today, the Chambers family knew little of and seldom discussed their father Garfield's family. Who they were, from where they had migrated, or what they had done had been pressing questions in my mind for many years. Why was so much more known about the Reese family than about the Chambers family? I went home the Summer of 1993 with one major goal in mind: to learn more details about Grandfather Garfield, his family, and what made him the outstanding family man and provider he was.

Sensing the urgency of my search for knowledge about Garfield, Uncle Clifford invited me to accompany him on a visit to Uncle Henry and Aunt Ida's home early on the morning of July 15, 1993. Immediately upon arrival, my questions began to fly, first to Uncle Henry, then to Uncle Clifford, and, occasionally, to Aunt Ida, who was most sympathetic with my cause. The uncles told me for the first time that Garfield's father was named Henry Chambers, for whom Garfield's second oldest son, Henry, is named. Garfield's mother was Bessie Corkell Lee. He had seven brothers: Walter, Horace, Marian, Ben, Jim, Albert, and Joseph. Lillie was his only sister. Aunt Ida knew Garfield's two aunts, Mag and Icum Corkell, very well and arranged for me to obtain a picture of both for this project.

Icum and Mag Corkell, Garfield Chambers' aunts.

According to the account given by Henry and Clifford, Garfield's father, Henry Chambers, was a gambler, who, by the standards of those days, was considered to be a "man of the world." His death was an alleged tragedy, a mystery that was never clearly resolved. Word had it that one night, while walking back home from a gambling match, Henry was struck by a freight train and killed. However, when his body was discovered early the next morning lying near the railroad track located not so far from where he lived, his solid gold pocket watch was missing. Speculations were made that Henry possibly had been attacked, robbed, and murdered by someone who tried to make it appear that he had been hit by a freight train. Although the Bastrop County Sheriff's Office conducted an investigation of his death, details of the case were sealed, and the mystery remains unresolved to this day. Regrettably, no accounts of Garfield's mother are available. Uncle Henry speculated that this lack of information may be attributed to the fact that his father, Garfield, seldom (if ever) talked to anyone about his own mom or dad. Unlike his wife Marie, Garfield was a very quiet person. He was an excellent listener.

Garfield Chambers was an incredible man. He spent many hours reading the Bible and the daily newspaper. He read both from the front to the back covers. Discussing world affairs and current issues was his favorite topic that dominated most of his leisure conversations with friends and with Mr. E.J. Their daylong conversations often concluded with plans for going hunting the next day. Squirrel hunting was an art with Garfield. He was the cleverest squirrel hunter I ever knew, with perhaps only one exception, his brother Marian.

Following many years of working the old Yancy Farm, Grandfather Garfield and the family moved to the St. John neighborhood in Austin. At the young old age of about sixty-eight, this man bought an old skinny-tire bicycle and rode it over twenty miles of dusty and hilly roads, daily, to and from his job of fence building at one of the largest palomino horse farms in North Austin. This bicycle was his only mode of transportation. I managed to secretly play with the bike often enough to learn to ride it by the time I turned nine years of age. Minnie, Jean, and several of the younger cousins also learned to ride Grandfather's old bicycle. After they had finished with the bike, I simply lost track of what finally happened to it. Garfield, however, never rode it again.

My curiosity about Grandpa Garfield's family members had continued to mount until the evening of December 8, 1999, when I first met Horace Lee, Ben Lee's son and Garfield's youngest nephew, currently living in Austin. Following our introduction by Cousin Marshall Toliver, Horace and I wasted no time getting acquainted. The first several minutes following our encounter were spent quietly staring at each other while the other cousins were talking. Our minds were telling us that we shared a common bloodline but had lived the first forty years of our lives without being aware of it. Horace Lee had provided a new linkage for me to discover additional members of the Garfield Chambers-Lee part of our family. Horace owns a successful tree service business in Austin, and we had so much fun servicing my mother's trees together. His next workday with me was spent visiting and meeting other members of Big Poppa's family.

Horace Lee

Twin sisters Mamie and Mary Chambers, nieces of Garfield Chambers and the daughters of Horace Chambers.

My uncle, Ben Lee, was an entrepreneur and the youngest brother of Garfield Chambers. Our circle of acquaintances continued to spread when I met several other members of the Ben Lee family a few months later. The most interesting thing I have learned to date about Ben's children is that most of them are successful business entrepreneurs as well. I visited the hair salon and clothing boutique owned and operated by wife Lula and daughter Rose. Daughter Shirley is the artist in the family.

Through our continued association and conversations, I will be meeting other members of Garfield's side of the family, and we will no longer be strangers to each other. Photos of the Ben Lee family members are shown below. ⚇

Rose, Shirley, Larry, Amber, Jeanniene, Crystal, Lula, and Abraham Lee

Pearlie, Rose, Shirley, and Jeanniene

Rose, Shirley, Amber, Lula, Jeanniene, Little Jeanniene, Twynisha, and Pearlie.

Obsequies for
Deacon James Arthur Garfield Chambers
St. Baptist Association Tabernacle
Monday, June 27, 1966, 3 p.m.

"A Grandfather's Farewell"

Garfield's sons and brothers

Garfield's wife, sisters-in-law, daughters, and other relatives

Garfield's sons and daughters-in-law, grandchildren, and great-grandchildren.

11

The First Grandchildren

(Fifth Generation)

Marie Reese married Garfield Chambers in 1903. They raised their twelve children together as husband and wife for sixty-three years, but they did not stop there. As grandparents, they also played a major role in the rearing of their thirty-six grandchildren, the first cousins. Preparing their lunches, walking some to school, baby-sitting others, and disciplining us all were never-ending tasks for them, but Big Momma and Big Poppa would have had it no other way. One standing rule Marie and Garfield had for their own children was that if they could not find someone with whom to leave their children, they should always bring them to their grandparents' home.

Raising a family of twelve in the early 1900s was a very challenging experience by anyone's standards, but the Chambers couple met this challenge head-on. All except five of the thirty-six grandchildren, Benzella Roberts, Minnie Hill, and Charles, David, and Don Chambers, are alive today. Of the remaining thirty-one, all, except five who have retired, are actively engaged in their chosen careers.

Although the primary Chambers family was balanced, consisting of six sisters and six brothers, our fifth generation of cousins is dominated by males who substantially outnumber females by a margin of 23 to 13.

Alfred Nash, senior of our fifth-generation line of cousins, is tall and dark and is thought by many to be the handsomest of all the males. He is a retired mechanical engineer. His brother Herbert is a reverend, the only one in this generation. Their two younger brothers, Melvin and Leonard, are very active in the trucking and transport industries. Doris and Erma Jean complete the Nash family by providing it with an array of beauty, kindness, and intellectual sensitivity. They chose nursing, business, and government as their respective fields of endeavor.

LaZelle Westbrook, a graduate of the University of California in the field of nursing, is a professor at San Jose State University. Her brother, Lt. Raymond Westbrook, had an exciting career with the San Francisco Police Department before retiring in 1998. The two have lived in San Francisco most of their lives. Ray travels extensively from California to Texas and South Florida. His hobby is ship cruising, and he takes a cruise annually.

My sister, Minnie Hill Taylor, was a veteran member of the Houston-Tillotson College managerial staff. Shortly after her only visit with me in Florida, she passed away on December 24, 1993.

Benzella Roberts, the first child born to the Roberts family, was also the first cousin of the group to pass on. She was a youthful forty-three when the Lord came for her on September 14, 1980. Best known and admired by her cousins and friends for her romantic and sentimental personality, Benzella was loved and admired by everyone who knew her. As a reward for the great

Benzella Roberts

love and compassion she always had for others, God blessed her by making her a proud mother of eight. Her sister Myra ("Tay") was career-oriented at a very early age. Immediately following graduation, Myra joined Southwestern Bell Telephone, where she earned the distinction of being one of the highest-ranked Black manager/supervisors within the company. Having completed thirty-five successful years with the company in November 1991, Myra became the first, and the youngest, of all the cousins to retire at the youthful age of forty-two. She also assumed the role of that of her own late mother as anchor "Super Lady" of the entire Roberts family. Myra and Benzella's two brothers, Bertrand and John Michael, graduated from high school and were employed by the U.S. Postal Service in Houston. In addition, they became interested in boxing. Both brothers married and had started rearing their families when they were threatened by a mysterious illness, which has imposed certain limited restrictions on both today.

Myra Fleeks cutting her retirement cake in 1991.

Jean Evelyn Allen Yates ("Tootie Ann") is somewhat unique in the Chambers Family Treasure. She grew up as an only child of the Allen family. As such, Jean tried to make a brother or a sister out of all of her cousins with whom she grew up around in St. John. During our early childhood days, she would often cry because her cousin Ray and I refused to let her hang around or to play with us whenever we were together. Consequently, Jean would often retaliate by reporting to Big Momma some of the devilish activities Ray and I enjoyed getting into, which always caused us to get a whipping. Jean grew up to become a professional schoolteacher in the Austin Independent School District (AISD) and an accomplished pianist who leads and directs several church choir groups. Through her active leadership in the AKA Sorority, her dream of having her own sisters is being fulfilled. Jean and Myra are often in touch with each other, as are Ray and I.

Helen "Tootsy" Chambers Patterson was the fifth consecutive girl to be firstborn among the Chambers siblings. Distinguished by her fair complexion and auburn hair, Helen grew up to become an educator and musician. Her sister Shirley, who now lives in Dallas, learned the skills of her mother and became a professional cosmetologist. Shirley is so beautiful that she could have been a model. Shirley and Helen have three brothers: Charles, Sam, and Michael. These three boys idolized their father Floyd, who taught them many business and trade skills at young ages. Upon completing his military duty and college, Charles embarked upon a career with the U.S. Postal Service, where he later became steward of the employees' union. Sam and Michael became interested in the field of computer technology. Michael has recently developed a hobby in music as a disc jockey. I call him "Mr. Mellow Fellow." We will have to check him out sometime before he gets too busy in his new career.

Willie Norris Jr. (r) with cousin, Jim Hill (l), at Elnora Chambers' memorial service, January 2003.

Willie Norris Chambers Jr. reversed the trend by becoming the first male child born to a Chambers sibling in over five years. Willie was an outstanding athlete in high school. Football and track were his specialties. Fascinated by automobiles, he easily learned to be a mechanic. Willie Jr. is currently struggling to overcome some personal difficulties which are among some of the most serious issues confronting the people of our generation. We are all praying for your successful recovery, Willie. We love you. Keep believing in yourself, and you can do it. Howard Chambers, the middle son in the family, has always played the role of the middle man. His younger brother, Paul, is an excellent air-conditioning and refrigeration technician who has found much delight in watching his sons grow up in sports. Their only sister, Delores, was always known for her quiet personality and beautiful, warm smile.

Marshall ("Butch") Toliver maintains the network hub of communication with all the cousins and other family members. His talents as an artist and sculptor, coupled with skills at boating, cooking, and entertaining, provide him with a level of versatility that is second to none. Marshall has been employed by the city of Austin as a traffic engineer and as a building code inspector/supervisor. In terms of a chronological pecking order, Butch falls exactly in the middle of the lineup. He is number 18 of the 36 first grandchildren of Marie and Garfield Chambers. He is enjoying his new home located in Roundrock, Texas.

Butch's younger brother, Ronald Toliver, is a business manager. In this capacity, Ronald has enjoyed the privilege of working in both private and public business institutions. He travels extensively but is most happy with his return to his native home state of Texas to establish with his wife their own private computer service business.

Henry Allen ("Dawg") Chambers, a professional electrical engineer, learned the basic skills of his trade from his late father, Seallen. His younger brothers, Kenneth and Roger, enjoy spending weekends together playing dominoes. Sometimes the game goes on all night. Their sisters, Kaye and Joy, also enjoy being together. Kaye is an administrative assistant with the County Judge's Office and travels to New Orleans to party whenever she gets the time. Joy favors her mother very much.

Several years had gone by since a new grandchild had been born to the Chambers family. When Dwight Chambers was born, he became the thirty-fifth first cousin of the family. Approximately three years following his birth, Nell Chambers was added to the family and became the thirty-sixth and the youngest of all the first cousins today. Could our Uncle Clifford possibly surprise us once again? ✖

Sisters Helen and Shirley checking out Texas

First cousins, James and Myra, with Myra's daughter Erica and grandchildren, Paige and Cameron.

The James Arthur and Marie Chambers Grand Family Reunion of 1997, reflecting the overall growth of the family over the past four decades.

Marie Chambers (center) with her crew of grandchildren, as of 1953

Kayla Williams, 11-year-old golf sensation of the South Florida community, great-great-grandaughter of Marie and Garfield Chambers.

12

𝕏 𝕏 𝕏 𝕏 𝕏 𝕏 𝕏 𝕏 𝕏 𝕏 𝕏 𝕏 𝕏 𝕏

The Great-Grandchildren

(Sixth Generation)

Unlike Marie and Garfield's first line of grandchildren, their great-grandchildren of the sixth generation almost doubled their predecessors. There are seventy-two individual members of this generation. Female members dominate. Moreover, the females outnumber males by almost the same ratio as males had dominated females in the fifth generation (37:34).

Having left home at seventeen years of age to attend San Francisco City College and to serve in the United States Air Force, I saw very little of my second cousin group members and knew only a few by name. These children were products of the 1960s and 1970s and strangers to most of the Chambers family members because the families had scattered to such far distances and seldom had opportunities to visit and to get to know each other. Both Grandmother and Grandfather Chambers would often express their regrets that they had spent such little time with their great-grandchildren. They would be proud to know that our annual family reunion is rapidly solving this problem and that education continues to be an important area of emphasis.

To gain some insight into the sixth generation, I elicited some firsthand perceptions in conversations with my own children, Eva, James, and Dudley. "When we hear stories about things our grandparents, uncles, and aunts did, we can see some of those traits in ourselves," says Dudley, a 1999 graduate of the University of South Florida. "Hearing all of them talking and telling stories about things they did as kids makes me realize that we might have the potential of doing some wonderful things ourselves," he said. In the conversations Eva had with my sister Minnie, she learned about the exciting experiences Minnie and I had as kids growing up in the country areas of Texas picking cotton and playing organized basketball in elementary school before boarding the school bus to attend high school in the city of Austin. Eva was able to see and to understand how living in the country and being bused to school in the city affected our lives.

Hearing my own children express themselves about their visits to Texas each year to attend the reunions has made me more aware of just how much they are developing a real sense of family history. It gives me great pleasure to know that they have experienced, and will continue to experience, some fond family traditions that might have otherwise been lost.

Rap music and breakdancing are popular art forms during this era, and video/computer technology has become standard equipment of this time. Some great-grandchildren of the sixth generation, however, have excelled in athletic, educational, and other professional skills far beyond the levels their great-grandparents would have dreamed possible. For example, one great-grandchild, alone, is both a captain in the United States Army and an emergency medical doctor. This simply was unthinkable in their day and time. Slavery had been abolished, and five generations had passed, but these remarkable achievements had finally been accomplished by one of their own great-grandsons of the sixth generation. Garfield and Marie would have been so proud to see this young man today and to hear him express his excitement about becoming a father for the first time.

Belinda Nash, a social worker, although not personally aware of her great-grandparents' devotion to serving the needs of others, experiences that good feeling they derived when she administers to the needs of her clients each day. La Shawn Nash, a vocalist, Belinda's cousin, experiences that joyful feeling through the songs she sings at church on Sundays with the same spirit and passion that were experienced by her great-grandparents decades ago while laboring in the fields. Terri Westbrook, a saleslady, has developed outstanding sales and marketing skills that might someday motivate her to open her own business. Terri did not know that her great-great-grandfather, Peter Reese, was a clever salesman and barterer who marketed most of the products he grew to obtain the goods and services he could not produce for himself. I think they would have enjoyed swapping sales pitches.

Florida Governor Jeb Bush congratulates Dr. James O. Hill II upon graduation from Nova Southeastern School of Medicine.

Traci Patterson and Eva Hill Taylor extend the number of family members choosing education as their careers. Five members of our family are currently schoolteachers. Diversity among sixth-generation members of the grandchildren is finally characterized in the person of Roderick Fleeks, law enforcement officer, who serves the City of Houston, Texas Sheriff's Department. Roderick is also a bodybuilder on the national competitive circuit.

Dr. James O. Hill II completed his medical residency training in July 2004 and was placed on active duty in the United States Army at Fort Rucker Army Base, located in Dothan, Alabama. He was later transferred to Fort Campbell to undergo combat training before his deployment to the war in Iraq on December 9, 2004. I had the sad honor of escorting my son, Captain James O. "Butch" Hill, to the deployment formation roll call that morning at "07:45 a.m." When his name was called, he boarded the bus and took a seat. I waved goodbye to the troops from my car until the bus rolled out of my sight and quietly wept.

While I have provided you with brief information about some of my second cousin members of the sixth generation in the foregoing paragraphs, I must honestly admit that more study and research must be devoted to this talented segment of the family. Important data and facts about this generation have not been collected that would suggest the ultimate impact of the prior generations on this distinct group and the impact this group might ultimately have on subsequent seventh- and eighth-generation family members. 〰

Dr. James O. Hill II off to Iraq

Father with son at the Roll Call Formation, December 9, 2004, at Fort Campbell.

13

The Great-Great-Grandchildren

(Seventh Generation)

The great-great-grandchildren of Garfield and Marie Chambers are products of the 1970s and the 1980s. At this time, there are sixty-eight great-great-grandchildren. In contrast to the sixth-generation predecessors, females continued to outnumber males but by a lesser ratio (i.e., 35:33). A female, Corbie Franklyn, was the first-born of the seventh generation. Corbie's mother, Diane Taylor, was the firstborn of the sixth generation.

My personal knowledge of most members of the seventh generation of the great-great-grandchildren dramatically drops. It is at this level and at the eighth level of generations where the Chambers family must increase its efforts to become more familiar with each other. Our failure to reverse this trend or to increase our knowledge about the members of the seventh and eighth generations could result in the loss of our Chambers family lineage for the generations to come.

In the old St. John community where I grew up, parents, teachers, and other adults took active responsibility in expressing consistent values and expectations. Because of their actions, most of the youngsters weathered the storms of adolescence and passed into adulthood rather successfully.

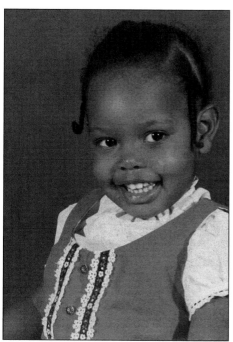

Corbie Franklyn, firstborn of the seventh generation.

By contrast, however, many of the members of the seventh and eighth generations are not as fortunate. They live in more modern-day communities which are often shaken by conflict, unemployment, poverty, and despair. Unlike my generation, today's adults, parents, and neighborhood institutions often do not take active responsibility in expressing consistent values and expectations. They do not provide sufficient or proper direction or hope for a brighter future. This, ultimately, causes these younger generations to become discouraged and confused, leading them to drift toward delinquency, crime, and unwed pregnancy.

In the twenty-first century, lifestyles are different. There is a lack of two-parent homes. There are many stepfamilies and half families. Children are left on their own because, whether they come from single-parent homes or two-parent homes, the parents have to work, many times, more than one job, to keep food on the table. There is more stress. More than ever before, education is critical to keep up with this fast-paced and technological existence. Living is very expensive. Life is not as simple as it used to be. Unfortunately, these seventh and eighth generations are greatly affected. It is time for adults, parents, and neighborhood communities to step up and to take responsibility for our future generations.

I believe that our family can do much to forge closer and stronger bonds between ourselves and members of the seventh and eighth generations. First, we might start by encouraging interfamily interaction within our family group as a whole. Second, we might encourage interaction with those families of the seventh and eighth generations in particular. The families of our younger generations should have an opportunity to learn from the families of our older generations. There is a treasure chest of family support available. Garfield and Marie Chambers instilled in our family the ability to reclaim and to control our children by being actively concerned and involved in their young lives. It is time for us to answer the call of the seventh and eighth generations and to continue the tradition of Garfield and Marie Chambers.

In his nationwide address on April 19, 1964, President Lyndon B. Johnson stated, "We have entered an age in which education is not just a luxury presenting some men an advantage over others. It has become a necessity without which a person is defenseless in this complex industrialized society . . . we have truly entered the century of the educated man" (Bornet, p. 169). Pursuant to Mr. Johnson's declaration, we must encourage our youth to strive to gain or to accomplish the best education possible. This pursuit should include knowledge of family history, culture, and academics. ✕

14

The Great-Great-Great-Grandchildren

(Eighth Generation)

A boy, Shamarchs Roberts, dawned the beginning of the eighth and youngest generation of the Garfield and Marie Chambers family. In reviewing the genetic pattern of this family for the past five generations, males have been the firstborn of the fifth and eighth generations. Females have been the firstborn of the third, sixth, and seventh generations.

Shamarchs Roberts

Viewing the American family groups as the most primary of social institutions, the fourth cousin, or eighth-lineage generation, has been most often looked upon as the last line of kinship in a given family. If this is true, we must then agree that greater efforts should be made to acquaint and to educate the members of this fourth-cousin generation as to their family history. It is equally important that the members of our earlier generations make similar efforts to get to know and to possibly influence the development of our last line of beloved members.

Truly getting to know one's relatives, as I see it, can only happen when there is meaningful social interaction occurring between the group members and individual members over a reasonable and continuous period of time. Activities such as our annual family reunion, which we have conducted since the passing of Big Momma in 1987, have been the Chambers way of ensuring such interaction. The Chambers Family Reunion of 1994 was perhaps our best example. Shamarchs and Pierra Roberts were prominently displayed and introduced at this affair while we awaited the birth of the latest family additions in the persons of Jasmin Lee Johnson and her brother Chester, as well as cousins Patrik, Tyler, Tavian, Empress, and Corey. As the nine eighth-generation children begin to know and to play with their peer cousins of this generation, they will hopefully start to make inquiries about older cousins and relatives of preceding generations.

There are three things that people long for in the world: life, meaning, and love. Everyone has the desire, that yearning, that passion to live a life that has meaning and love within it. These three desires are free for everyone. It was Christ's mission to come into the world, to endure suffering, and to die so that every one of us could satisfy and achieve these three longings. Marie and Garfield would often say, "We, as Christians, are Christ's representations in the world today, and we, therefore, should never forget that mission. We all have to give life, meaning, and love to our family, friends, and neighbors. By accomplishing this mission, our family would grow beyond these eight generations to be linked with immortal generations."

15

Grandparenthood

(Jim Hill's First Experience)

Grandparenting for Garfield and Marie Chambers was a vocation. Based upon what I can remember and from my own observations, it appeared that these two grandparents were far more protective of their grandchildren than of their own children. Every grandchild responded to this safeguarding in his or her own very personal way. I dreamed of becoming a grandparent someday myself and of copying all the unique skills I saw them applying among our family group. If I could perhaps learn to master their skills with half the level of success they experienced, I would consider myself a success according to any measure of standard.

Now that my own children have become adults and parents in their own right and have started their own careers, I felt that I was ready to assume the role of a grandparent. The big question, however, was whether I could be as successful at this role as Garfield and Marie.

My return to Austin the Summer of 1990 was a mixture of both happiness and sadness. A brother-in-law, James Mosby II, had passed away seven days before the marriage of his youngest brother, Gerard, who had just completed his medical internship to begin medical practice. I was honored by presenting Gerard's beautiful bride, Lanetta, at the wedding. This was also the thirty-fifth anniversary of my Anderson High School Class of 1955. Aunt James had passed away. Aunt Alberta was recovering from an extended illness, and Aunt Ida was slowly eroding in a nursing home. My search for unidentified members and pictures had continued for the third consecutive summer, but with all of these episodes, I knew I must hasten to bring this project to a close.

Then, on December 20, 1990, I was the victim of a major auto accident, which temporarily impaired my neck, back, and right hand. I subsequently underwent treatment for a mild heart disorder. Shortly thereafter, our daughter Eva got married. This combination of major events demanded my fullest attention and served to further delay the completion of this book for several additional months. By this time, it was summer again.

The Summer of 1991 provided yet another opportunity for the Chambers family to assemble in Austin. This was truly a summer of reunions. Our Chambers family, the L. C. Anderson School Grand, and the L. C. Anderson Class of 1956 reunions were all held in Austin during the Fourth of July holiday weekend. These occasions offered me an opportunity to capture photographs of our family and friends that have served to enrich and to broaden the scope of our family experience. My dream of someday becoming a grandpa became a reality on July 23, 1991, when our daughter Eva gave birth to a beautiful little girl named Kayla Marie Williams. Her grandmother and I could hardly wait for the Summer of 1992 to come so that we could take her on vacation with us to meet her relatives in Texas, as well as friends all along the way. It was now time for me to take the path toward becoming the best grandpa I could be.

Our first grandchild, Kayla Marie Williams, 8 months.

The Summer of 1992 was a thriller! To begin with, the City of Fort Lauderdale honored me with the celebration of a "Jim Hill" Day Festival in Lincoln Park on June 20. On this same date, the Broward County Government planted a Memorial Oak Tree in St. George Park in recognition of the role I played in promoting beautification projects in cities throughout the county. Kayla's first visit to Disney World and the wedding of a long-time friend, Cheryl McDermott, in Orlando, Florida, on July 4, were the first stops made on our way to Texas that year. Our son Jim bought his first car, a 1992 Saturn. We spent an exciting weekend at Richard and Grace Mosby's beach house with our parents, brothers, sisters, and children in Galveston, Texas. Dudley caught a 9 1/2-pound catfish at Rainbow Lake in Austin, his largest ever. Renovating the old car shed built by my dad and me in the early fifties was very rewarding to me. We also witnessed seeing Kayla take her first steps during this vacation and my mother Ethel taking her first ride aboard a ferryboat. Although no Chambers family reunion was held this year, the addition of Kayla to our treasure was evidence that the Chambers family was still alive and growing. ✣

Chambers' Family Reunion
June 29, 1991, Decca Lake Park, Austin, Texas

The six remaining Chambers children (back row, l to r): Cliff, Bernice, Mary, Ethel, and Henry; (front row): Alberta holds Paige Fleeks (youngest third cousin).

Family members assembling for photographs

Sisters Alberta, Mary, and Ethel (center) surrounded by all first cousins of the Chambers family

Chambers sisters and brothers joined by sisters-in-law, Lillian and Allene.

Chambers second cousins relaxing at the Reunion Picnic

Hills' Summer of 1992

Kayla at the Magic Kingdom

Eva, Kenneth, and Kayla

Grandparents on the ferryboat in Galveston, Texas.

Jim II's car

FIRST STOP
Disney World, Orlando, Florida

Kayla's first visit to Disney World, July 3, with Grandparents Jim and Eva Hill.

Father Dione and Commissioner Ed Kennedy at the Jim Hill Memorial Oak Tree in St. George Park, Fort Lauderdale, Florida.

Granddaughter Kayla, Grandpa, and Uncle Jim.

SECOND STOP
The McDermott Wedding, July 4th, in Orlando

Little Girls Grow Up: Cheryl and Eva

Family's weekend at Richard and Grace's beach house in Galveston, Texas.

Hill family's sendoff to end Vacation 1992

16

Family Demographics

(Jim Hill's Perspective for Viewing The James Arthur Garfield and
Marie (Reese) Chambers Family Generation Lineage Today)

As the grandson of the late James Arthur Garfield and Marie (Reese) Chambers, I have taken an even closer look at the Chambers family, viewing it from the oldest- to the youngest-known generations today. Although in the preceding chapters, I have shown and described the interfamily working relationships within this group, I now invite you to focus with me on the eight generations of our family to see some of the rather revealing dynamics of the group. Tables 16.1, 16.2, and 16.3, below, have been developed to enable one to view and to follow a variety of genetic, chronological, and biological trends characteristic of the Chambers family members as they have occurred throughout the generations.

First, illustrated in Table 16.1, is the lineage of the James Arthur Garfield and Marie (Reese) Chambers family from the oldest- to the youngest-known generations today spanning the period of approximately 1800 to 2002. The names of our known relatives who are representative of the generations identified have been included as a meaningful person of reference for future dialogue.

Table 16.2 shows the biological and genetic trends of the Chambers family, characteristic of members belonging to the fourth through eighth generations. These five generations were selected for analyzing because they are the ones with whom the majority of our living relatives are most familiar.

Finally, Table 16.3 is a chronological listing of the births and the deaths (where applicable) of Garfield and Marie Chambers, along with their twelve children. The longevity of each member has been included to emphasize the historical tendency for a significant number of its members to live well beyond eighty years of age. Birthday anniversaries are included to encourage everyone to celebrate and to remember each one's birthday with a card, flowers, or a call. ⚏

Table 16.1: Lineage of the Chambers Family from the Oldest- to the Youngest-Known Generations

Generation Number	Representative Names	Date of Birth	Date of Death	Longevity
First	Miriah Reese	1800	Unknown	Unknown
Second	Peter Reese Lilia (Baltimore) Reese	1869 1847	March 1932 August 1957	63 years 110 years
Third	James Arthur Garfield Marie (Reese) Chambers	1885 1884	June 1966 July 1987	81 years 103 years
Fourth	Ethel (Chambers) Hill	1913	March 2001	88 years
Fifth	James O. Hill	1936		67 years
Sixth	Eva M. (Hill) Taylor Kenneth Williams	1966 1965		37 years 38 years
Seventh	Kayla M. (Taylor) Williams	1992		11 years
Eighth	Patrik Roberts	1997		6 years

Table 16.2: Chambers Family Biological and Genetic Trends Belonging to Members of the Fourth through Eighth Generations

Generation Number	Birth Total	Birth by Gender M	F	Firstborn M	F	Death Total M	F
Fourth	12	6	6		x	7	4
Fifth	36	23	13	x		2	2
Sixth	72	35	37		x	1	2
Seventh	68	33	35		x	0	0
Eighth	9	5	4	x		0	0
TOTAL	197	102	95	2	3	10	8

Table 16.3: A Chronological Listing of the Chambers Family Members Reflecting the Date of Birth, Death, and Longevity of Each Member

Name	Date of Birth	Date of Death	Longevity
Marie Chambers	May 7, 1884	July 29, 1987	103 years
James Arthur Garfield Chambers	March 12, 1885	June 24, 1966	81 years
Alberta Nash	October 30, 1906	March 19, 1997	91 years
Leon Chambers	February 4, 1908	April 9, 1977	69 years
Henry Chambers	May 7, 1911	December 31, 2001	90 years
James Ada Roberts	March 6, 1912	November 9, 1989	77 years
Ethel L. Hill	January 17, 1913	March 30, 2001	88 years
Mary Westbrook	June 22, 1914		
Norris Chambers	August 27, 1915	April 11, 1978	63 years
Thelma Allen	May 27, 1918	October 13, 1980	62 years
Seallen Chambers	March 17, 1921	April 22, 1988	67 years
Clifford Chambers	September 9, 1923		
Floyd Chambers	September 4, 1925	July 6, 1978	53 years
Bernice Toliver	August 22 (Yr. confidential)		

17

The Tree of Life

(A True Statement of Beauty)

J. F. Houck's poem *The Tree* describes poetically what the lives of Garfield and Marie Chambers meant to us.

"A barren place this earth would be
If God had failed to plant a tree
Along the pathways where we walk
Lost, with love, in friendly talk.
Or if on mountains reaching high
No trees were banked against the sky.
Suppose a tree could never make
Its face reflect on placid lake,
Or cast its shadow on the stream
Where lovers often stroll to dream,
Or Autumn leaves were never made
And none upon the grass were laid?
If valleys, hills and dales, were free
Of grass and flowers, but a tree
Grew there, that spot would be
A paradise for you and me.
For weary there, we'd find sweet rest
Beneath its shade be kissed, caressed.
If birds could never build a nest
Within a tree's protecting breast,
Or weary from their flight on wing
Could never stop a bit to sing,
A dismal place this earth would be
without God's masterpiece, the tree."

From the Chambers' union sprang twelve branches. From these twelve branches grew numerous subbranches, which I have identified in Chapter 4. Foliage of these branches and roots casts a vast shadow covering a span of eight generations. Each member of the Chambers family has been identified and described by me based upon my personal knowledge and relationship with each.

Primary attention has been focused upon the twelve Chambers sisters and brothers and upon the first cousins so that the younger members of our family might become better acquainted with their older kinfolk. Only through knowledge of our early ancestors can we fully begin to understand and to appreciate our present and future family roots.

The Chambers family has made a long journey from farms, woods, and bottomland to urban communities throughout the central, eastern, and western areas of the United States. The hardships and the triumphs of our early ancestors have served to encourage and to motivate each of us today. Most of our second, third, and fourth cousins have grown up having only a faint recollection of their adventurous rural heritage and gallant ancestors. The people we meet in school, at work, or at play cannot appreciate our background because they know so little or nothing about it.

My life for the past thirty-five years has been spent in the cities, schools, offices, and social gatherings of some of the finest people I have ever been privileged to encounter. Many have allowed me to enter their homes, their lives, and their hearts. My hope is that this project has allowed them and other readers to learn about my extraordinary grandparents, Garfield and Marie Chambers, whose lives have had such a great influence on the lives of each of our family members, but especially mine.

Throughout their lifetime, Garfield and Marie placed major emphasis on Christianity and the church and the need to keep these two forces active in one's daily family life. Although not based entirely on their own personal experiences, education and learning are the avenues to achieving success and to living a peaceful, respectable, and productive life. "Herein lies the wisdom of the emancipated," they advised, both now and then.

Garfield and Marie's dreams and aspirations for their family became their treasure. As their family became their most valued treasure, so too, must our own families remain the central focus of our lives as well. Their plight from being sharecroppers in Wilbarger to becoming landowners and homeowners in Austin was a dream that became a reality through hard work and perseverance. Keeping their family together socially and physically during times when separation was the norm for Blacks, rather than the exception, was their greatest challenge. Having successfully lived together as husband and wife for sixty-three years before Grandfather passed away was an example of the love and the stability they had hoped for their children, grandchildren, and great-grandchildren in the years that lay ahead.

Garfield and Marie Chambers were proud Black Americans who pioneered the development of their St. John neighborhood, its community school, and Blacks Memorial Baptist Church. In recognition of their lifelong parental influence, the 197 offspring of this great couple have memorialized them through a variety of personal achievements and accomplishments. Six offspring became professional educators; six, professional managers, directors, and administrators; four, businessmen; four, engineers; six, outstanding high school and college athletes; one each, a clergyman, a mason, a police lieutenant, an artist-sculptor, and a medical doctor; and, finally, two musicians. The Chambers family legacy and treasure will remain forever. ⚊

Great-great-granddaughter Kayla Williams, 8-year-old junior championship female golfer of the year 2000, Okeeheelee Junior Golf Foundation, Wellington, Florida.

A FAMILY TREE PROJECT

Artistically designing a tree that might symbolically depict the growth and the development of this family through eight generations was indeed a major challenge for me. Marshall Toliver possessed the talent to do it, but the time required to do so became a prohibiting factor. The principal of Dillard High School in Fort Lauderdale, however, arranged an interview for me with Joshua Jenkins, a very talented junior drawing student at the school. Following a brief explanation of my project, Joshua enthusiastically accepted the task of drawing a tree that he felt would be most appropriate for our family. Without hesitation, I assigned him the project.

Having given the project further thought, Joshua felt compelled to explain why he had accepted the challenge with such great enthusiasm. He gave the following explanation:

> My name is Joshua Jenkins. I am a junior at Dillard High School in the School of Performing Arts. I maintain a 3.5 GPA. I enjoy drawing, singing, and playing football, but drawing is where my heart is. That's all I've done since I was about three years old. I grew up in a single-parent home with my older brother. As a child, I was always surrounded by strong women who helped raise me. My great-grandmother was one of the people who left an impact on my life. Not only was she my grandma but also she was everyone else's grandma too. When things got rough, she turned to God to help her keep things right. I come from a strong Christian background. I believe this is what keeps the people in my family strong.
>
> This tree means so much to me because I believe in family and knowing where you came from, not just physically, but spiritually. We came from a long line of proud, intelligent, active people. I believe our race is tremendously more stronger than any other race. Throughout the tree are what I perceive to be ancestors. I drew thick roots and branches that spread to represent the strength and longevity of a people. I wanted to make the tree as detailed as possible to show that it's unique and one of a kind. Drawing this family tree inspired me to really trace my family back. I believe that people with large families are blessed and should cherish that. I also believe that people with small families should hang on to each other and be grateful. We all gain knowledge and become better people when we learn about our roots. I truly thank you, Mr. Hill, for this opportunity to develop the Chambers Family Tree.

I am most grateful to Joshua Jenkins for volunteering his visionary and artistic talents to create the Chambers Family Tree for this book. Talent and family values expressed in this family tree project that were developed by Joshua are quite reflective of the caliber of youth who are leading us into the new millennium. ✠

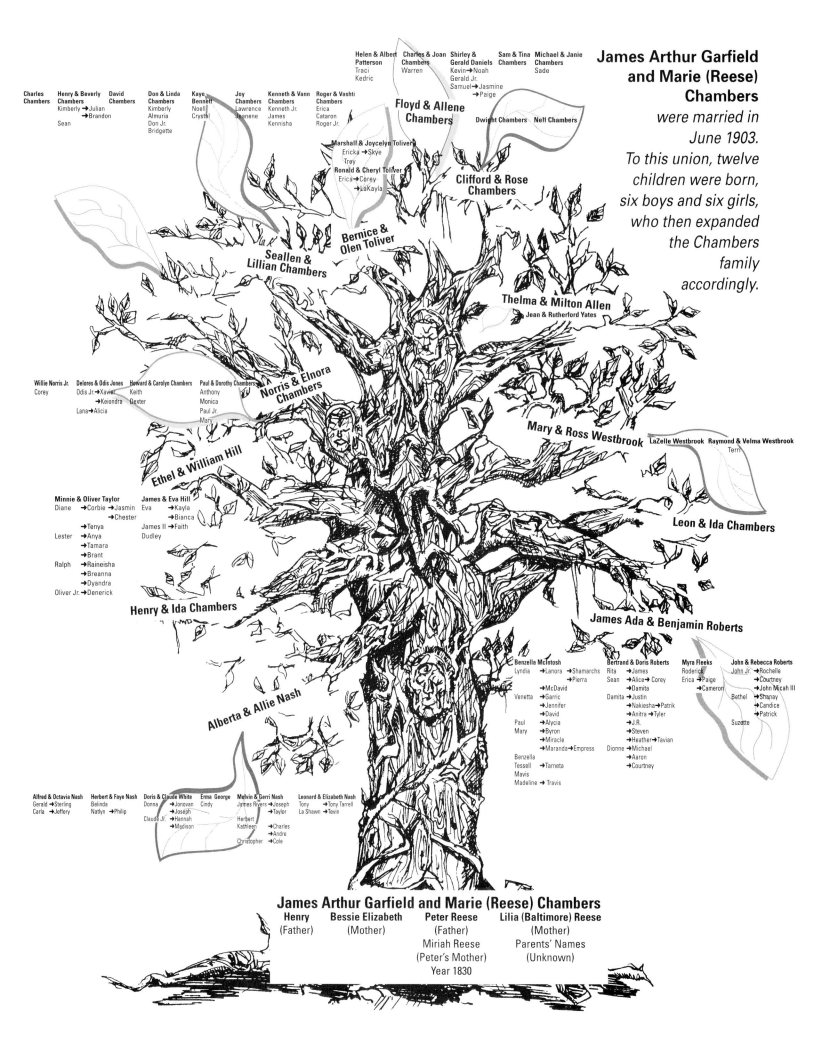

James Arthur Garfield and Marie (Reese) Chambers *were married in June 1903. To this union, twelve children were born, six boys and six girls, who then expanded the Chambers family accordingly.*

Floyd & Allene Chambers

Helen & Albert Patterson
Traci
Kedric

Charles & Joan Chambers
Warren

Shirley & Gerald Daniels
Kevin ➜ Noah
Gerald Jr.
Samuel ➜ Jasmine
➜ Paige

Sam & Tina Chambers

Michael & Janie Chambers
Sade

Dwight Chambers   Nell Chambers

Charles Chambers

Henry & Beverly Chambers
Kimberly ➜ Julian
➜ Brandon
Sean

David Chambers

Don & Linda Chambers
Kimberly
Almuria
Don Jr.
Bridgette

Kaye Bennett
Noell
Crystal

Joy Chambers
Lawrence
Jeanene

Kenneth & Vann Chambers
Kenneth Jr.
James
Kennisha

Roger & Vashti Chambers
Erica
Cataron
Roger Jr.

Clifford & Rose Chambers

Marshall & Joycelyn Toliver
Ericka ➜ Skye
Trey
Ronald & Cheryl Toliver
Erica ➜ Corey
➜ LaKayla

Bernice & Olen Toliver

Seallen & Lillian Chambers

Thelma & Milton Allen
Jean & Rutherford Yates

Willie Norris Jr.
Corey

Delores & Odis Jones
Odis Jr. ➜ Xavier
➜ Keiondra
Lana ➜ Alicia

Howard & Carolyn Chambers
Keith
Dexter

Paul & Dorothy Chambers
Anthony
Monica
Paul Jr.
Mary

Norris & Elnora Chambers

Mary & Ross Westbrook

LaZelle Westbrook   Raymond & Velma Westbrook
Terri

Ethel & William Hill

Minnie & Oliver Taylor
Diane   ➜ Corbie ➜ Jasmin
➜ Chester
➜ Tenya
Lester   ➜ Anya
➜ Tamara
➜ Brant
Ralph   ➜ Raineisha
➜ Breanna
➜ Dyandra
Oliver Jr. ➜ Denerick

James & Eva Hill
Eva   ➜ Kayla
➜ Bianca
James II ➜ Faith
Dudley

Leon & Ida Chambers

Henry & Ida Chambers

James Ada & Benjamin Roberts

Alberta & Allie Nash

Benzella McIntosh
Lyndia   ➜ Lanora ➜ Shamarchs
➜ Pierra
➜ McDavid
Venetta   ➜ Garric
➜ Jennifer
➜ David
Paul   ➜ Alycia
Mary   ➜ Byron
➜ Miracle
➜ Maranda ➜ Empress
Benzella
Tessell   ➜ Tarneta
Mavis
Madeline   ➜ Travis

Bertrand & Doris Roberts
Rita   ➜ James
Sean   ➜ Alice ➜ Corey
➜ Damita
Damita ➜ Justin
➜ Nakiesha ➜ Patrik
➜ Anitra ➜ Tyler
➜ J.R.
➜ Steven
➜ Heather ➜ Tavian
Dionne ➜ Michael
➜ Aaron
➜ Courtney

Myra Fleeks
Roderick
Erica ➜ Paige
➜ Cameron

John & Rebecca Roberts
John Jr. ➜ Rochelle
➜ Courtney
➜ John Micah III
Bethel ➜ Shanay
➜ Candice
➜ Patrick
Suzette

Alfred & Octavia Nash
Gerald ➜ Sterling
Carla ➜ Jeffery

Herbert & Faye Nash
Belinda
Natlyn ➜ Philip

Doris & Claude White
Donna   ➜ Jonovan
➜ Joseph
Claude Jr. ➜ Hannah
➜ Madison

Erma George
Cindy

Melvin & Gerri Nash
James Rivers ➜ Joseph
➜ Taylor
Herbert
Kathleen   ➜ Charles
➜ Andre
Christopher ➜ Cole

Leonard & Elizabeth Nash
Tony   ➜ Tony Tarrell
La Shawn ➜ Tevin

James Arthur Garfield and Marie (Reese) Chambers

Henry	Bessie Elizabeth	Peter Reese	Lilia (Baltimore) Reese
(Father)	(Mother)	(Father)	(Mother)
		Miriah Reese	Parents' Names
		(Peter's Mother)	(Unknown)
		Year 1830	

18

Shadow of a Grandmother

(A Mentor)

Marie Chambers, age 36

In every family, there seems to be only one grandchild who possesses the social, physical, and emotional traits of the grandparents more than anyone else. Among Marie Chambers' thirty-six grandchildren, the late Minnie Hill Crothers, my sister, was probably the one.

Marie Chambers was a very good-looking and well-built woman. There was never any doubt who was in charge of her family and her household. Although she experienced her fair share of hardships, disappointments, broken promises, and shattered dreams during her lifetime, I never once heard her weep or saw her shed tears about anything. She was a person of action who was never hesitant to make a hard decision. Patience, perseverance, and compassion: Marie Chambers had it all. My sister Minnie was blessed with the same traits, and much more. Our cousin Myra Fleeks shared so many of these traits as well.

Minnie L. Hill Crothers, age 17

Minnie Hill Crothers was born on March 9, 1935. She was a year older than I. She was preceded in death by our stepfather, Eugene Hill, and also by her biological father, William Hill, in 1989. Minnie professed a faith in Christ at eleven years of age and was baptized at Blacks Memorial Baptist Church in Austin. She later affiliated with New Hope Baptist Church. She married Oliver Taylor in 1953, graduated from Anderson High School in 1955, and moved to Homestead Air Force Base, Miami, Florida, where she lived as a U.S. military family for approximately fifteen years. To this union, four children were born.

Minnie L. Hill received master's degree with honors.

Upon her return to Austin in the late 1960s, Minnie underwent some rather difficult family and domestic life readjustments. However, as a single parent and head of the household, while educating herself, raising and educating her four children, and managing the business affairs of our elderly mother, she aggressively pursued a professional career in education and business administration. She earned a Bachelor of Arts in Business Administration from Huston-Tillotson College in 1974, a Master of Education in Counseling and Guidance from Prairie View A&M University, Prairie View, Texas, in 1979, and completed a Teacher Certification in Business Education in 1985.

Minnie served on the Huston-Tillotson College management and faculty staff from January 1968 to 1993 in a variety of progressively responsible capacities, including Secretary in the Upward Bound office, 1968 to 1969; PBX Operator, 1969-1970; Mail Clerk and Central Store Operator, 1970-1974; Supervisor of Mail and Duplicating Services, 1974-1979; Teacher, Maplewood Community School, 1980-1982; College Housing Director, 1986-1989; and Academic Counselor/ Coordinator for the Upward Bound Program, 1987-1993. Through the above capacities, Minnie was instrumental in educating, motivating, and molding the lives of thousands of youths and college students throughout Austin and the United States. Most regrettably, however, a declining health condition mandated her early retirement in April 1993, thereby culminating twenty-five years of loyal service to the college she loved so dearly.

(l to r) Minnie, James, Ethel (Daughter, Son, and Mother)

As a member of New Hope Baptist Church, Minnie tried to practice her religious faith on a daily basis through loving and serving the many needs of her own children, the family, and others. She was the recipient of seven major honors and awards, including the National Business League Women of Distinction Award in 1988.

She left in joyous celebration to cherish her memory: her loving children, Diane, Lester, Ralph, and Oliver Jr., of Austin; nine grandchildren; two great-grandchildren; a son and daughters-in-law; a devoted mother, Ethel Hill; one proud and admiring brother and his wife, Eva Mosby Hill; a niece, Eva Taylor; two nephews, James II and Dudley Hill; three grandnieces, Kayla Williams, Bianca, and Faith Hill; two half sisters, Mary and Ann; four half brothers, William Jr., Edward, Dan, and Tommie Hill of Austin; one stepsister, Mrs. Jean Freeman; three aunts; two uncles; thirty-five cousins; seventy-two second cousins; sixty-eight third cousins; and nine fourth cousins.

Minnie was a role model to me. She would challenge me to the maximum. She always had a way of somehow convincing me that I was a much better competitor in anything than I ever thought I was. "Your small stature," she said, "should never keep you sitting on the sideline, James." One grade ahead of me in secondary school, Minnie watched everything I did and was usually the first person to approve or disapprove of anything or any action I undertook. Both Minnie and I played on the Fiskville Elementary School girls' and boys' basketball teams. She was a star on the girls' team, while I was a sub on the boys' team and only played when my team was safely ahead of the opponent. Minnie was leading scorer and could make baskets from any position on the court. Always poised, ladylike, and competitive, she possessed all the basketball skills I wished I had. An honor student herself, she would insist that I also make the honor roll. In high school, I only let her down once, by making two A's and three B's during my senior year.

My first experience running for an elected position happened during my sophomore year (1953) at Anderson High School where Minnie insisted that I run for president of the student council against two outstanding upper classmen, Betty McAdams and Verna Belle Wicks. Minnie was confident that my leadership and speaking ability, coupled with my popularity, would enable me to defeat my opponents. Obviously, my sister Minnie became self-appointed campaign manager, made all the posters for the race, and organized all of my support groups in all classes. With my sister's hard work,

I came within three votes of winning the presidency. It would have been the first such victory for a sophomore in the history of the school.

I thought my loss would have been too much for my sister to bear, but her reaction was quite the opposite. As soon as the results were announced on the public address system, Minnie rushed to my homeroom to congratulate me. "Good job, little brother," she said. "We ran a good race and lost this time, but wait until next year and you'll take it all." Win I did, in 1954, even by a landslide! Minnie was the one who made it all happen. I tried hard to never let her down.

Whenever Minnie was invited to a party, Mother always insisted that I go along with her. I think we were the only brother and sister required to do this in the neighborhood. All the girls were taller and older than I. Minnie never complained about Mother making me accompany her to the parties, but she would always make me dance with the girls no matter how much taller they were than I. This is how I first learned to dance and really socialize. Minnie was responsible for it all. I wish that every boy could have a sister like my Minnie. Her grandmother, Marie Chambers, was mighty proud of her also.

In recognition of her twenty-five years of outstanding service to the school and her community, her name is listed in the Huston-Tillotson College Hall of Fame in Austin. ⚙

The Capitol at Austin, Texas

Austin, Texas, honors Black Achievers

The Hills' darkest hour

Family and friends bid final farewell to Minnie

Mother Ethel preparing to return home accompanied by John Fletcher and Diane Taylor.

James and family bid Mother Ethel goodbye before returning to Florida.

19

Visions of the Emancipated

(Homeownership a Reality)

Garfield and Marie Chambers were both children of former slaves who had been freed. Their mothers and fathers were children of free African descendents who had been brought to this country by slave marketeers and sold to plantation owners. They were, therefore, accustomed to moving from one farmland to another. Their homesites were also temporary. Mothering and fathering their twelve children under such conditions was an art the Chambers were forced to master during some of the most trying times for Black people in the history of our country. The lack of ownership of the lands and houses they worked and occupied for so many years made it that much harder to get ahead in life and to experience the emotions of being a free people. In spite of the hardships they faced, however, Garfield and Marie's visions of someday owning their own land and home never faded, but, in fact, grew stronger with each passing year.

Norris Chambers, WW II Veteran

When over half of their children had grown, were drafted by the military, or enrolled in college or high school in one of the big cities in Texas, it became even more difficult for the Chambers to make a decent living on the farm where they lived in Wilbarger County. Incredibly, this family had managed to overcome the crippling effects of World War I (1914-1918) and the dramatic challenges of the Great Depression (1929-1940) without having to live on charity. They never had to feel angry or humiliated by anyone because they had learned how to support themselves the hard way. Like many other people who lived and worked for others during these unforgettable periods of our country's development, the Chambers no longer trusted their farm lord to protect their social welfare. They had finally lost faith in the philosophy of sharecropping which they and their ancestors had labored under for so many years.

Floyd Chambers, High School Student, 1945.

Living frugally, Garfield and Marie managed to save a little money. A few months passed. One day at the end of November 1938, during a meeting held with his sons in the front yard of their farmhouse, Garfield decided that the time had finally come for him and his family to leave the Yancy Farm, which was then owned by Leon Rivers, a local banker. Pursuant to this decision, Garfield, while attending the St. John Christian Association held annually in Austin, heard about the cheap land sales going on in the St. John neighborhood where lots were being sold for $50 each. He purchased two of them from the Reverend A. K. Black, who owned most of the land in St. John. Shortly thereafter, Garfield

Rev. A. K. Black

began to construct a house on the property. Garfield and his family were now on their way to owning land for the first time in their lives!

Clifford, the next-to-youngest son of the Chambers family, left home on the Yancy Farm to go live with Cousin Mamie Pleasant so he could oversee and coordinate construction of the new house with the carpenter and to prepare for the family's historic move. When his father became ill, Clifford would drive the family's old 1931 Plymouth back and forth between St. John and the Yancy home place daily to make sure that construction of the house was progressing satisfactorily.

The Chambers family moved to the St. John neighborhood, First Addition, in 1939, where they enjoyed owning and developing their own property. To the Chambers, moving into their new home in St. John was something like the experience His Holiness Pope John Paul II once described as "crossing the threshold of life." For this family of freedmen and women, the full impact of the emancipation of Blacks had just become reality. Freedom, human rights, and a new sense of dignity were being felt by this family who had performed the "hard work" and who had achieved "ownership" of their land and home as was advocated by Booker T. Washington. St. John was the Chambers' "promised land," and they had finally reached it.

Although I was quite young at the time, I can recall that my grandparents brought with them from the farm a cow, some pigs, and a few chickens. The self-sustaining lifestyle they had been accustomed to for most of their lives was continued at their new home place. St. John was a rural community at that time where animals were permitted. Several families in the neighborhood owned animals as well.

Old Fiskville Road, 1939, is now Highway I-35 and still divides St. John's First Addition and Second Addition neighborhoods.

The First Addition of the St. John community consisted of but two long, unpaved gravel streets, Blackson Avenue and Delmont. It had been many years, but I could still name the families who lived along each street. Fiskville Road, now Interstate Highway 35, was the only dusty, gravel road passing through and dividing the First and Second Additions of the St. John neighbor-hoods. V. K. Black's general store, where everyone bought candy, kerosene fuel, and gasoline, was the first building located on Blackson Avenue. The Black home was located adjacent to the store. Other homes along the street included the Chambers, Emanuel Hill, Junious Scott, the Jacksons, Pleasants, Roberts, Whites, Reeds, and Landrens. Along Delmont were the Kings, Dixons, Turners, James Dean, Madison Brown, Howells, Collins, and, finally, the pride of the neighborhood, Fiskville School.

Garfield and Marie Chambers became well-known and well-respected by everyone in the neighborhood, perhaps not so much for being one of the early settlers but more because the Chambers would stake their milk cow on the vacant lots throughout the neighborhood every day to graze. Children would line the streets to see Grandmother lead her cow back home every evening for milking. Many times, I would be running along behind Big Momma and the cow. The Chambers provided milk and butter to many neighbors on a regular basis. Sharing their farm products with the neighbors had been a common practice of the Chambers family everywhere they had lived. They considered it to be the only right and neighborly thing to do. Someone once said that "you can take some people out of the country, but you can't take the country out of them." My grandparents were good examples. The spirit of giving and sharing became a family trait which has been practiced by each generation.

Two of St. John's oldest homes (approximately 70 years old).

When Garfield and his family had finally settled in their new home in St. John, they became strong advocates for the community. First, they started to encourage their own sons and daughters to purchase land and to build homes in the neighboring Second Addition. Two daughters, Ethel and Thelma, and five sons, Leon, Norris, Floyd, Clifford, and Seallen, were successfully recruited. Their son Henry and daughters Alberta and James Ada chose Austin, Elgin, and Houston, respectively, as their hometowns. Mary settled in San Francisco, while Bernice, the youngest of the Chambers siblings, remained at home. Once all the Chambers children had married and had begun to settle down, the grandchildren population grew like wildfire. Marie and Garfield became instant baby-sitters for all of them. They were becoming parents all over again, except, this time, it was for their fifth generation. These proud grandparents felt as responsible for raising and educating their grandchildren as they had their own twelve. They were as quick to discipline this fifth-generation group as they were their own fourth-generation kids.

Every grandchild of the fifth generation had experienced the scrutiny and the wrath of Big Momma and Big Poppa at one time or the other. It was an experience one could never forget. Just hearing about our disciplinary experiences with these grandparents was enough to keep the sixth and the seventh generations going straight.

The Chambers' concept of child abuse was the exact opposite of the concept people have today. According to the Chambers' version, "the failure to administer physical discipline and counsel to the child when required constitutes 'the child abuse.'" One major result of the Chambers' philosophy of discipline is that the children and the grandchildren whom they disciplined have seldom, if ever, spent time in jail and have been successful and proud, law-abiding citizens. ☒

20

Support for Education and Educators

(The History of Fiskville Elementary School)

James Arthur Garfield Chambers believed in education, knew the value of education, and was always supportive of the educational institutions located within his community. Grandmother Marie Chambers was equally supportive of the neighborhood school and all the faculty members who worked there. In fact, for several years, Mrs. Thorn, Wilbarger's only teacher at the time, was a boarder in their home. Mrs. Thorn had to teach Grades 1 through 8 in this one-room little school located about a mile from the Chambers home.

Although the school had no kindergarten class, Mrs. Thorn allowed me to attend school at five years of age, along with my Aunt Bernice, for half-day sessions, until being picked up by my grandparents. Through this early experience, I developed a great love for school and for my teachers.

The Chambers family moved to the St. John community in 1939. To enable my sister Minnie and me to be closer to a school facility, our mother arranged for us to spend weekdays with our grandparents in St. John, where we attended Fiskville Elementary School from Grades 1 through 8.

The love I had already developed for school and for learning at five years of age flourished the first day I attended Fiskville Elementary School. Big Momma and Big Poppa, Mother, and Mr. E.J. always encouraged us to take part in everything we could at school. They supported everything we were a part of, even when they sometimes did not quite understand what we were doing.

My first teachers, Mrs. Phillips, Ms. Dodson, Mrs. Cooper, and Mr. Battle, taught us well and provided us with an educational foundation, a sense of loyalty, pride, and respect for the school, teachers, church, and the community that have remained throughout the years. According to their educational philosophy, one's educational process must involve the home, school, church, and the

Mr. and Mrs. Edward J. Battle (1954), with their 1950 Ford, used to transport as many as eleven basketball players to games throughout Central Texas.

Fiskville St. John's Faculty: (l to r) Miss M. E. Lewis, Fourth Grade; Mrs. M. D. Strong, Third Grade; Mrs. Della J. Phillips, Second Grade; Mr. Edward J. Battle, Sixth Grade; Ms. N. J. Dodson, Fifth Grade; and Mrs. S. A. Upshaw, First Grade.

community. Academically, I was always among the high achievers. Always the smallest boy in the group, Mr. Battle coached me into becoming an outstanding softball player and a member of the varsity basketball team. Mr. Battle was my first athletic coach, and he introduced organized competitive sports to all of us at Fiskville. My greatest fan was Grandfather Garfield, who attended all of our home games and rooted for me with a great, big smile. Big Momma helped organize the school's lunch program and volunteered many hours each week preparing the food. I graduated from Fiskville on June 1, 1951, without ever knowing how the school got started. Forty-six years later, I learned the story. It was most fascinating.

Through the assistance provided by Mr. and Mrs. James E. Mosby, retired educators and school volunteers of the AISD, a historical account of the creation of Fiskville Elementary School had become a reality. Well-known for their many years of civic, educational, and charitable services to the Austin community, this dedicated couple contacted the AISD on my behalf and obtained official records of exactly what I needed to know in order to provide a historical account of the school's commencement.

According to records obtained from the AISD, undeveloped land currently located at the northwest corner of Delmont Avenue and Highway I-35 in the St. John community of the city of Austin was originally owned by Mr. John H. Mulkey and Susan Mulkey.

Fiskville School building renovation and addition of 1953

Motivated by a need to have an elementary school facility to serve this predominantly Afro-American district in this unincorporated area of Austin, Community School Trustees near Fiskville in Little Walnut Creek purchased 0.50, or one-half acre, of land (21,780 sq. ft.) from the original owners for the low price of only $5.00. The average cost of land per acre at the time was only $10.00. This land purchase was filed on December 28, 1867, at 9:00 a.m., and was recorded in the Public Records at 10:00 a.m.

Fiskville School, now St. John, was established in 1934, and was located in Fiskville Common School District No. 11. The late Mrs. Sarah Russell was the first principal. She was succeeded by Mrs. Della J. Phillips.

Responding to this apparent need, on May 31, 1941, Trustees (Mrs. C. D. Harvey, Jr. Robinson, and Carl Rundberg) of Fiskville Common School District No. 11 purchased an additional 0.66 acre (or 28,749.60 sq. ft.) of land from the John H. Mulkey heirs (23 signings) for the total price of $75.00. The average cost of land per acre at this point in time was $11.64. This sale was filed for record on June 10, 1953, at 4:50 p.m., and was recorded on June 11, 1953, at 8:50 a.m. With the purchase of this land, there was now just a fraction over one acre of land to utilize. An additional building was constructed, and minor renovation work was done on the original building.

During these early recording years, the Fiskville Common School District No. 11 and the Summit Common School District No. 18 were consolidated for reasons not apparent in the records. However, on August 28, 1952, approximately two

Mrs. Della J. Phillips, Principal at Fiskville School.

years before passage of the 1954 U.S. Supreme Court decision ending segregation in public schools, the superintendent of the Austin Board of Education, Mr. Carruth, presented the negotiations for the Fiskville School property to the Board for consideration. Mr. Porter, a participant in the negotiations, reviewed the matter as outlined in his memo to Mr. Carruth, dated August 28, 1952, and recommended that the Board of Education purchase the Fiskville Elementary School and land from the Fiskville School Board for $9,609. A motion to this effect was moved by Mr. Prentice and was seconded by Mr. Lamme that the recommendation be adopted.

The motion passed unanimously. On August 10, 1953, following further clarifications, payment was made to the Summit School District as voted. Fiskville Elementary School had become the property of the Austin Public School System.

At a time when the city of Austin was experiencing its most rapid growth in residential and business populations, and with a need to improve its major roadways and to expand its northern jurisdictional boundary, more attention than ever before had begun to be focused upon Fiskville Elementary School and the surrounding neighborhood. In my opinion, passage of the 1954 U.S. Supreme Court decision was a clear mandate for the Austin Public School Board to drastically upgrade the Fiskville School facility. The wood-framed, underlighted, ill-equipped, overcrowded, substandard buildings with two outdoor toilets, that had been our pride and joy for so many years, were no longer acceptable. A change was coming, a change that the people were willing to accept, but only with mixed emotions.

Well abreast of the social and the political implications that all the above developments would have on the City and the School Board, Mr. Broad presented a letter from Mr. H. C. Jernegan at a school board meeting offering $4,000 for the old Fiskville site and buildings. After a discussion of the fact that bids had been called for twice and all bids had been rejected as being far under the appraisal of $4,000.00, Mr. Gary moved acceptance of the offer of Mr. Jernegan. The motion carried. It was sold on May 12, 1958. Fiskville Elementary School, the institution that had won a special and permanent place in the hearts of all who had ever attended it, was, at last, history.

Fiskville Elementary School closed its doors in 1958. The ramshackled building of 1952 was demolished soon thereafter. A modern, new red brick facility, St. John Elementary School, was constructed about a mile up the road overlooking the old Fiskville school site, now a Days Inn Hotel. The new school had five classrooms, a lunchroom, indoor toilet, tile-covered floors, bright lights, and freshly painted pastel-colored walls, the kind of facility I would have been thrilled to attend. However, an ultramodern facility such as Pickel Elementary School, built for the St. John community in early 2000, was simply unimaginable.

Jim Hill, a graduate of Fiskville Elementary School in 1951.

A graduate of Fiskville Elementary School, and as one grandson of the late Garfield and Marie Chambers whose young mind was prepared for adulthood by a faculty whom I loved deeply, respected, and fully supported, I will always cherish the love and the memory of Fiskville School and its teachers.

Attending Anderson High School was something I had always looked forward to, but with much anxiety. Could I successfully compete with my urban contemporaries? Would that competitive spirit Mr. Battle kindled within me at Fiskville continue to grow at Anderson High School? These were questions constantly on my mind. Fortunately, I got off to a good start at Anderson, making the honor roll each year. I selected football as the only sport in which to participate, was inducted into the student honor society my sophomore year, became president of my junior class, and president of the student council my senior year.

Big Poppa never learned the game of football, and I suppose that is why he never attended football games to see me play. He and Mr. E.J., however, attended all of my softball and baseball games and also took me to see the Brooklyn Dodgers, the New York Giants, and the Cleveland Indians whenever they came to Austin. They both swore that I would someday be the next Roy Campanella. The three of us would often go on hunting and fishing trips together. Going to the Huntsville Rodeo and to the Ritz Theater to watch championship boxing and Western movies was our favorite pastime. Only the three of us would attend these activities together. We always had a great time, and they taught me many lessons about work and how to handle myself in relating to others.

The support and the leadership demonstrated by Garfield and Marie Chambers as responsible parents and grandparents forged a strong bond among themselves, their family, the community, and the school, which bond was never broken. They are the role models we must try to emulate in rearing our own families today.

A sampling of students, teachers, and staff of Fiskville Elementary School is shown below.

Joe Dean

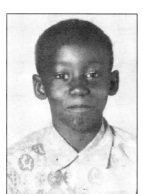
Buddy Jackson

Jean Allen, Third Grade

Mrs. Beatrice Dean

Members of the last graduating class of Fiskville School before its closing in 1958: (l to r) Ruby Scott, Easter Jackson, and Jean Allen.

Mrs. Cooper

A group of well-dressed students of Fiskville School.

A special singing group of students of Fiskville School.

Wilma Turner

21

Family Reunion, 1993

(The Biggest and the Best Reunion Ever)

Brothers Clifford (l) and Henry (r) Chambers display their awards received for barbequing service.

Everyone had looked forward to the 1993 Chambers Family Reunion. With two major organized reunions under our belts in recent years, we all had the feeling that the 1993 gathering could possibly be our best. Regardless of the weather, location, or time of year, nothing could have possibly made us feel any different.

Considering all things, it had been an exciting year for most of us, but on the other hand several family members were faced with serious illnesses. Uncle Ross Westbrook, for example, had traveled the farthest to attend the affair. Relying on a wheelchair and an oxygen tank, Ross was joined by a host of Westbrooks from Elgin, who, after many years of living in California, were returning to take up permanent residency in

Ross Westbrook (wheelchair) with members of the Westbrook family.

their native home of Texas. My sister Minnie was still trying to get over her exciting visit to Florida, taken back in March, to visit my family and me. She had made the trip with Mother, who experienced her first airplane flight. It was Minnie's first visit to my home since we became adults and her first visit back to Florida since departing from Homestead Air Force Base over thirty-five years ago.

Cousins Jean Yates (l) and Erma Jean (r) cooking up fish.

A big Friday night fish fry signaled the beginning of the 1993 Chambers Family Reunion. Hosted by the Tolivers, the event was made possible through the fishing skills of Bernice and other members of the Chambers family who had fished Austin's Rainbow Lake for the past several months. This occasion set the stage for the most successful reunion our family had ever witnessed. Cousin Erma Jean George had moved back to Texas from Seattle; Ray had met a new, exciting friend from Washington, D.C.; and several newly born cousins were scheduled to meet the family for the first time. Everyone was ready to have fun.

The excitement of this reunion could be observed in the behavior of both young and old alike. To begin with, Jean Yates, mistress of ceremony for the program, locked her keys in the car immediately upon arrival at the picnic held at the Bergstrom Air Force Base Park. My granddaughter, Kayla Marie Williams, two years of age, and her mother Eva arrived at the picnic from Florida just in time to meet all the family members. They were followed by Myra Fleeks and all the family from Houston.

(back row, l to r) Michael Young, Madaline Young, M. McIntosh, Nickesha Roberts, MacDavid McIntosh; (front row, l to r) Myra Fleeks, Travis Young, Chakka (friend of M. Roberts), Justin Roberts, and J.R. Roberts.

Every cook in the family had put forth his best efforts in preparing a most delicious dinner. No picnic of ours would be complete without the tasty barbecue prepared by Uncle Clifford and Uncle Henry the day before. When the crowd of over two hundred relatives had assembled, the program began. Aunt Sis (Bernice Toliver) welcomed everyone; a prayer of thanksgiving was offered by our cousin, the Reverend Herbert Nash; and songs of praise were led by Cousins Helen Patterson and Jean Yates.

Rev. Herbert Nash offering prayer.

(l to r) Bernice, Jean, Rutherford, and Helen leading the songs.

Historical Garfield and Marie Chambers family T-shirts were designed and worn by all family members as an appropriate tribute to their legacy. Each individual family group, however, selected a different shirt color to help identify his own immediate family members. Pictures of Garfield and Marie were prominently displayed on the back. Prizes were given to the family having the most family members present at the picnic. The family which traveled the longest distance to attend the reunion also received special recognition. With the attendence of recently born cousins of the seventh and eighth generations at this year's reunion, it was evident that the Chambers Family Treasure was alive, well, and still growing. It was a thrilling experience to have my granddaughter Kayla join me in updating the family on the progress being made on this book. Milia McShan Goins represented the McShan family, while Rev. Sam Reese provided additional visibility of the Reese heritage to which Big Momma belonged. This predinner program planned by the committee was so very entertaining. It was a great show from start to finish, but, much to our surprise, the real drama of our program happened during the dinner.

Jean Yates presents an award to Rev. Sam Reese.

Milia Goins and Eva Hill

When it was finally time for dinner, the line formed quickly. Everyone was hungry. The food servers were few, carving knives for the meat were scarce. We suddenly recognized that we had obviously failed to plan effectively this phase of the program. I was summoned to fulfill the role of meat carver/server of the food line. A serving crew consisting of Doris and Erma Jean, Bernice, and Jean Yates, Uncles Henry and Cliff, Charles Chambers, my wife Eva, and me quickly adjusted to the crisis, and the group was fed on time. Everyone had all they could eat and more. We all departed from the reunion picnic with nothing but good thoughts and feelings about everyone and a commitment to get together again real soon. ✠

The food line R-U-S-H

LaZelle Wesbrook and Adel Scott

Jim Hill and Mother-in-Law, Eva Mosby.

Venetta McIntosh's winning smile.

Joy Chambers adorning tree

Warren Chambers, "Bass Master."

LaZelle Westbrook takes prize for the most family members attending reunion, 1993.

Jean embracing the Toliver family.

Rev. Sam Reese and Henry Chambers, first cousins, reminiscing about old times.

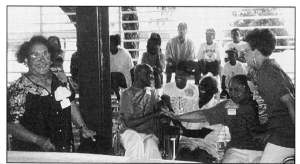

Ethel Hill (l) enjoying laughs with the Westbrook brothers and Joycelyn Toliver (r).

Eva, Kayla, Jim, and Kimberly chatting

Leonard and Herbert Nash, Rutherford Yates, and Albert Patterson.

Kaye Bennett remembering her dad.

Mary Lucy McDonald

The Floyd Chambers Family pause for the cause.

The Nash Family

Bernice, Eva, Ray, and Jean

Myra

Alfred, Cliff, Ruby "kicking back"

Relatives just checking things out

Charles remembering his dad

133

1993 Reunion Highlights...A Cousin Affair

Traci, Dudley, and Tanita

Shirley, Jean, Helen, and Minnie – first cousins. "Go Girls!"

Ann and Jim (a serious romance in bloom).

Joycelyn, Eva, Marshall, Oralyn. "One big hug-in for all."

Cousins Jean Yates (l) and Octavia Nash (r)

Roderick with Cousin Cindy

1993 Reunion Highlights...Family and Friends Alike

Minnie and LaZelle visited by a friend.

Bernie, James, Eva, Hattie, Dudley, and Tanita.

Milia, Bernice, Idaree, and Jim with granddaughter Kayla.

Jean and Myra show off award.

Dwight toasting the moment.

Ethel with grandson Dudley

Helen thinking it over

22

We Met, We Asked, We Talked, and We Learned

(Knowledge Through Family Interaction)

Since that first family reunion held in 1979, the Chambers had gradually begun to know and to interact with each other on an intergenerational basis. Exactly why it had taken our family so long to achieve this level of comfort in our social interactions remains a puzzle for many of us today.

The 1994 Chambers Reunion was not just another one of our regular annual family get-togethers. The primary focus this year was on mixing, meeting, and greeting. Every individual made it a point to spend some real time with those relatives we knew least about. Everyone seemed more willing than ever before to exchange questions and information about themselves and their immediate family members. No matter how focused the conversation became on the families, however, all would ultimately relate to the significance of our grandparents, Marie and Garfield Chambers, and the influence each had had on all of us.

Mrs. Mosby, Bernadette Kaye, Ray Westbrook, and Naomi White.

Mary Mosby Bacon and Venetta Mackey

Ethel Hill and niece, Myra Fleeks

For the second consecutive year, I had volunteered to carve the meat and to be one of the servers. My Texas chef's apron made me feel so good to be home with my family once again. My mother-in-law, Mrs. Eva Mosby, and sisters-in-law, Mary, Bernadette, Gloria, and Naomi, all joined with my family and me in celebrating this great legacy honoring Garfield and Marie Chambers, who had always valued having close relationships with those family members who have joined our family through marriage.

James with mother-in-law, Eva Mosby.

Jean Allen Yates represented the whole family on this occasion by giving a special salute to the two remaining Chambers brothers, Henry and Clifford. Both had been among the chief planners of the annual reunion since its inception. The Roberts family members travel from Houston each year to continue their mission of getting to know their relatives. Myra Roberts

Members of the James A. Roberts Family

Fleeks proudly explained to her aunt, Ethel Hill, how happy she was to see how much of her family has learned about their relatives over the past several years through the reunions.

LaZelle Westbrook and Adel Scott

Ethel and Mary

Members of the Roberts family huddle

Alfred and Ruby Nash

LaZelle Westbrook, of San Francisco, discussed with her cousin, Adel Scott, the joys of belonging to a large family. Sisters Ethel Hill and Mary Westbrook recalled the days they spent together growing up as little girls and dressing their sons and daughters like twins. Younger members of the Roberts family found it amusing to see how the family members entertain themselves through simply talking to each other. Alfred Nash and wife Ruby were quite relaxed when spending this special day together with the family. Alfred is the oldest of the thirty-six grandchildren of Marie and Garfield Chambers. To all of us, Alfred is the "Billy D. Williams" of the family.

Mary Mosby chatting with Clifford Chambers.

Alberta Nash, Leonard Nash, and Ethel Hill

Erma Jean Nash and Alberta Nash

Mary Mosby chatted with Clifford Chambers; Leonard Nash entertained his mother, Alberta Nash, as well as Aunt Ethel; and Erma Jean Nash expressed the joys of being with her mother and family after living in Seattle for most of her young adult life. Erica, Nell, Kevin, Mayerland, and I formed a cousin's strong line while Cousin Joy Chambers checked us all out. Mrs. Mosby and Mrs. Westbrook held a conversation on the sidelines while Bernice Toliver gathered her female nieces and her second cousin, Cookie Reese, around the dining room table for a brief smiling contest. Ronnie Toliver, of Dallas, chatted with his first cousin, Alfred Nash, about their experiences in the world of business and about retirement life.

Kevin, Mayerland, Jim, Nell, and Erica

Joy

Every time I would see Aunt Allene and her family huddling together, I could feel the presence of my late uncle, Floyd Chambers, who was the youngest son of the Chambers family. He passed away

Eva Mosby and Mary Westbrook

Alfred Nash and Ronnie Toliver

(l to r) Erma Jean, Doris, Cindy, Eva, LaZelle, Cookie, Jean Yates, Bernice, and Helen.

at a relatively early age, but his family continues to share the love and the warmth he always generated among the family. Rev. Sam Reese, of San Francisco, was presented a trophy for having traveled the longest distance to attend the 1994 reunion. He is one of several nephew ministers who Marie Reese

Allene Chambers family

Chambers felt so blessed to have in her family. Although Aunt Ida and Uncle Henry Chambers had no children of their own, they always shared the ownership of their thirty-six nieces and nephews, as did Henry's brother, the late Leon Chambers, who also had no children.

Venetta Mackey, second oldest daughter of our late first cousin, Benzella Roberts, should have won a trophy for having displayed the most glamorous personality of all. In spite of her handicap, Venetta conversed with everyone. Dressed all clad in her brown straw hat and purple Chambers memorial T-shirt, Venetta charmed us all with her beautiful, warm smile and thrilling conversation. Her sister Lyndia, Benzella's oldest daughter, really came to know her aunt, Mary Westbrook, and cousin, Helen Patterson, better than ever before. Warren Chambers, a product of the sixth generation of Chambers, was overwhelmed to learn just how numerous his family members are. Kevin, Gerald Jr., and Samuel Daniels, of Dallas, discussed

Sam Reese and Jean Yates

Ida and Henry Chambers

Warren Chambers and Aunt Helen Patterson.

Venetta and Aunt Mary

Lyndia Roberts and Aunt Mary Westbrook.

school and athletics with the cousins from other parts of Texas and Florida. Garfield and Marie Chambers had a number of grandsons who were better-than-average athletes in a variety of sports. The Daniels brothers, Jim II

Kevin, Gerald, and Samuel Daniels

The Hill family members

and Dudley Hill, and Don and Willie Norris Jr. Chambers were outstanding athletes and academic scholars as well.

Our cousins, Crystal, Noell, and Kaye Chambers Bennett, and Joy Chambers, would have made their late grandfather, Seallen Chambers, so proud to see them all growing up together and exhibiting the beauty and the charm for which both of their parents were so well-known. Although my sister Minnie had passed away, Ethel, Diane, Corbie, my wife Eva, and I all stood together as a family in remembrance of her.

Crystal, Noell, and Kaye

The 1994 Chambers Family Reunion was about to come to a close. We were approaching that sad moment when we would have to say goodbye. We paused at this time, however, to remember the deceased members of our family who had given so much of their lives to make possible what we all have to enjoy today. We have neither forgotten that some of them were indentured servants nor that others were slaves. We are the emancipated; we are the freed. The candles lighted on the flowers planted in memory of our deceased warmed the spirits and refreshed all of our souls. In God we trust. We trust that our cousins will be there to serve us food again next year. We know that the Nash family will continue to huddle in the absence of their late mother, Alberta. The efforts by my wife and me were applauded for continuing to support education for our children. The Mosby family and friends were also applauded for always taking the time to be with the Chambers family. This is the only way Marie and Garfield Chambers would have wanted it to be for the family. ⚹

Leonard Nash and Rutherford Yates: Ready to serve the food are Albert Patterson and Alfred Nash.

Members of the Nash family huddle

Jean presenting plaque to Eva and Jim in support of education for children.

Long-time friends relive the moments

138

The Chambers Annual Family Ritual for
Remembering the Deceased Members of the Family

Floyd Chambers

Thelma Allen

Rev. and Mrs.
Benjamin Roberts

Seallen Chambers

Ross Westbrook

Minnie Hill Taylor

23

Treasured Friends

(It's What Life is All About)

In every community where they lived, the Garfield Chambers family became well-known and well-respected by everyone who knew them. They were legends in Wilbarger Community and became pioneer settlers of the St. John community, being among the first ten families to build and to own their home around 1942. To the Chambers, the family always remained the focus. Whether at work or at play, members of the Chambers family could always be seen doing things together. Sundays, holidays, and daily meals were always major and special occasions to engage each other in visiting, family discussions, or just sharing the ups and downs of our daily lives. This tradition of family entertainment continues today.

Marie and Garfield Chambers valued their friendships with others. Butchering their livestock, harvesting the crops, canning and preserving their fruits and vegetables were always activities where friends were asked to join them. Their sick and disabled friends could always plan on being visited by Garfield and Marie. Sharing one's goods, services, and time was what friendship meant to them. It was their stewardship.

Although extremely proud of their Black heritage, the subject of being Black was almost never a major frame of reference in conversations with family or friends. Big Momma once told me that she married Grandfather Garfield because he was not as dark brown as she. I learned to believe that my grandmother was color conscious, especially as it related to the appearance of the offspring.

Big Momma would often emphasize how completely equal people are, regardless of race, creed, or color, and that I, as a Black person, must never consider myself to be greater or lesser than my Caucasian, Asian, or Native American contemporaries. Big Momma instilled this philosophy in all of her children and grandchildren. I grew up believing in her philosophy and to this day have never departed from it. The world is full of friends. We meet them everywhere we go and in whatever we do. Friends, to me, are like flowers and plants; they are all so beautiful to look at and to be among. The more you cultivate and care for them, the more beautiful they become to you, and the better they can make one feel, even on the gloomiest day of your life.

Paul McDermott, a professional colleague and copioneering director of Boys Clubs, once asked me, "How can you seemingly feel so comfortable socializing and conversing with Caucasians, especially with those considered to be of the affluent or wealthy class?" My response was simply that I considered Caucasians to be just ordinary good people, the type I enjoy being associated with as friends. I never judged such people by the material goods they owned, but, rather, by the quality of friendship they generated. I think all friends and people should be judged this way because friendships can last forever.

Throughout my lifetime, I have been blessed to meet so many different people who have become my dearest of friends. Having lived away from my immediate family and relatives since seventeen years of age, these friends became like family to me. They have enabled me to avoid the loneliness that one sometimes experiences when living so far away from the primary family. I know that my grandparents would have been proud to have met them all, but, unfortunately, my grandparents were unable to travel to visit me. These friendships and acquaintances will always be treasured.

Garfield and Marie would often say that people are judged by the friends and the company they keep. If this statement is true, I would surely like for my grandparents to know that during my lifetime, we were loved by many people and friends wherever we lived and traveled. We learned to value our friends just as they did. There were many lessons to be learned from our grandparents, but the greatest lesson of all that I learned is that there is no substitute for a true friend, and true friends are made in all colors. You find them at school, play, at work, church, in the neighborhood, the city, the states, and throughout the world.

I wish that our friends could have met my two adorable grandparents. They would have felt the mighty strength of their spirits. They would have heard the comforting words of wisdom they spoke, saw the wrinkles in their faces, and the scars on their hands from their many years of hard work and worries about the future. Big Momma was large in stature, weighing about two hundred pounds and standing only 5 feet 8 inches in height. One was tall, and one was short, but this odd-sized couple was a perfect match. Marie's nephew, the Reverend R.J. Reese, once said, "A church is never judged by its size but by its spirit." So it was with our grandparents. I have tried all my life to learn to be just like them in every possible way.

The following pages of this chapter include photographs of some of the most influential friends in my life and with whom I have ever had the pleasure of being associated. I have included these people because they will always remain dearest to me and a symbol of what I think friendship should mean to every human being. Their friendship and presence in our lives shall continue to shape my destiny. ✂

Jim Hill's School Friends • Best Friends • Life Friends

Horace and Rebecca Dixon, Austin, Texas, schoolmate, Grades K-8 at Fiskville School, St. John.

Albert Walker and wife, Austin, Texas, high school football teammate, Anderson High School Yellow Jackets, 1951-55.

Harold Hill and wife, San Francisco, California, college roadrunner, San Francisco City and State Colleges, 1955-58.

Leon Weaver and wife, Bowie, Maryland, fellow sociologist at Howard University, 1962-64.

Dr. Bobby Drayton and wife, Baltimore, Maryland, roommate at Howard University, 1962-64.

Clifford Hatchett, Eva Hill, and William Lee.

Anderson High School Class of 1953

Front row (l to r) Bobbie Robinson, Mary Robinson; back row (l to r) Juanita Houston, Lois Newby, and other classmates.

Donald Spence and Virginia Greg, Anderson Class of 1951.

Anderson High School Classmates, Class of 1956 (l to r) Lola Hawkins, Agnes Hill, Lois Newby, and Eva Hill.

Relatives and friends relaxing after big meal

(l to r) Eva Mosby, L. Britton, Mary Bacon, Eva Hill, and Pinky

Roots of Texas • High School Classmates

My St. John schoolmates, Marie and Josephine Dukes, with husbands.

Eva with her mom and dad and Creola Shaw at the All-School Reunion Banquet, June 28-30, 1991.

Dorothy Ates and Robert Fennell

Eva's Anderson High School Class of 1956

Wright, Coach Britton, and me at the Anderson Reunion Golf Tournament.

Josephine Wilson with classmate Eva Hill.

Anderson Yellow Jackets football teammate Albert Walker, and wife, with Eva.

Joyce Arnold Edwards

Anderson High School classmates Jim Hill grew up with in Austin, Texas, when schools were segregated

The Spirit of Texas

Minnie Hill

Jim Hill, Donald Spence, and Virginia Greg

Teny, Jim, Horace, and Rebecca

Eva and Bonnie

Miss Southern University, Eva Hill, 1988.

Ed, Eva, Alice, Elizabeth, and Dudley

Anderson Teachers Who Made a Difference

Eva Mosby and Mrs. Britton.

Mrs. Verna Arnold

Coach Britton with Jim Hill

Mrs. Brisby

Dr. King

James Mosby

Friends After College: Career Beginners and Family Starters

Dr. Romando and Ella James, Clemson, South Carolina, Jim's roommate in Newark, New Jersey.

Paul McDermott (r), Orlando, Florida, Boys Clubs of Broward County Pioneer Directors, 1966-1970.

Harold and Bernice Pearson, Fort Lauderdale, Florida, neighbors and educators with Charanda Striggles (standing).

Dennis and Nell Jackson, Fort Lauderdale, Jim's Easter Egg Hunt, 13th year.

Jackie, Bernice, Eva, Jim, and Edward's daughter at Charmette Party.

State Senator Mat Meadows and wife May, St. George Catholic Church members.

Alonzo and Tina Bembry, Newark, New Jersey, neighbors

Miriam Oliphant, Broward County School Board member, Fort Lauderdale, Florida.

Jim and John Hill, Fort Lauderdale, Florida

Oscar Reed (l) and Al Brown (r), at Charmette Celebration.

Ruth Phillips, Dania, Florida

Alcee Hastings (r), U.S. Congressman, Fort Lauderdale, Florida.

145

Friends and Family of St. George Church

Jim Hill, Bill Hutchinson and daughter, Jim II, and Beckie Williams fellowshipping after church.

Joseph Valmond, Father O'Shaughnessy, singer Rahiem "GQ," Father Chris, Kayla and Jim enjoying Sunday evening visit at the Hill home.

May Meadows (center) was Director of St. George Senior Day Care Center, 1985-1993.

Father Clements, Washington, D.C., greeted by Eva and student.

Bob and Jim were cochairs for the St. George Parish Festival in 1996.

St. George Parish Softball Team, 1985-1990

Pallbearers for Charlie Brown's funeral in 1995

146

Friends and Family of St. George Church

Rita was Parish House Assistant

Wilhemina and Margaret dance at the International Festival.

Maude and Roselyn

Dorothy and Ricardo at Black History Celebration

Muriel Lowe and Rosemary (center) serving dinner at Charlie Brown's funeral.

Father O'Brien departing from St. George Church

Church musician Berto, and wife, at church dinner

Close Friends and Acquaintances

Former First Lady Barbara Bush with Eva and James Hill

Eva meets Mr. Cab Calloway

Jim Hill presents key to the City of Fort Lauderdale to Ms. Earetha Kitt.

Race Car Driver Mario Andretti (rear, right) joins members of Midtown Business Association at Boys and Girls Clubs 1999 Dinner Auction; Mr. and Mrs. Jerry Carter (l) and Milton Jones (r).

Jim Hill presents key to the city to Jim Nabbie (original Ink Spots)

Movie and TV star Angie Dickinson with Jim and Eva Hill.

Dr. and Mrs. Erwin Vasquez, editor/owner of El Heraldo News.

U.S. Senator and Mrs. Bob Graham

Jim and Eva with Mr. Ed Bradley, 60 Minutes TV personality.

Eva Hill (l) with Wayne Huizenga, owner of the Miami Dolphins football team, and Elizabeth Hill.

Eva Hill, Miss Southern University 1985, welcomed back home by Fort Lauderdale Mayor Jim Naugle and Southern University Quarterback Club.

Close Friends and Acquaintances

Eva Hill and daughter Eva, with the Charmettes of Broward County, sponsors of the Annual Ebony Fashion Show.

Mr. Levi Henry, Publisher/Founder, Westside Gazette.

Jim Hill (center) greets Southern University delegation in Tampa, Florida.

Sylvia Poitier, Broward County Commissioner (2d from left), with Jim and Eva Hill and daughter Eva, at the Annual Boys and Girls Clubs Auction, 1999.

Miss Southern University, Eva Hill, with U.S. Congressman from Louisiana and company sponsor.

High school football stars 1954-1955: Miller, Upshaw, Hill, and Moten.

The Hill children's evening with boxing champ Mohammad Ali, 1978, in Miami, Florida.

Fort Lauderdale Citizens Board of Recognition: (l to r) U.S. Congressman E. Clay Shaw, Mayor Robert Dressler, Mayor Jim Naugle, Former Mayors Pete Clements, Porter Reynolds, and Robert Cox.

Living Examples of the Garfield and Marie Chambers' Meaning of Family Friendships

James and Lottie Caldwell family, San Francisco, California; St. Louis, Missouri; and Oklahoma City, Oklahoma.

Paul and Betty McDermott family, Orlando, Florida, and Boston, Massachusetts.

Harold and Bernice Pearson family, Lake City, Florida, and Atlanta, Georgia.

Ron and Ella James family, Florida, New Jersey, and South Carolina

The John H. Hill family of Fort Lauderdale, Florida

The Collins family, Austin, Texas, at the home of Bill and Cecilia James, in Pembroke Pines, Florida.

A Celebration of Families Among Friends • April 20, 1999

Four short hours following the City of Fort Lauderdale Commission Meeting honoring Jim Hill as Exemplary Employee of the City for 1999, the James Hill family hosted a dinner party at their home for two hundred of their closest friends and supporters just to thank them for being their friends. Photographs were taken at the celebration. ✖

Skip Johnston welcomes Bernice Toliver to city with an award.

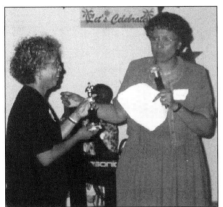

Maude Pearson presented Dr. Wilhemina King with a trophy for her role in St. George Passion Play during Easter Week.

Ruth Phillips presents an award to Rosemary McQuay for her retirement.

Linda Gill (c) presents sculpture to Harold and Bernice Pearson honoring their retirement.

(l to r) Mayor and Mrs. William Bantom and Hon. Franklin Sonn, South African Ambassador to the U.S., with the Hills at the Mayor's Ball, 1999.

Jazz musician Rocky Davis and vocalist Sammy "D" Denoms provided live entertainment for the evening.

Mrs. Striggles presented Ben and Becky Williams with the "Good Neighbor" award.

24

Godparenting

(An Act of Love)

It was Saturday morning, April 27, 1997. I received a long-distance call at 2 a.m. from Mary Westbrook informing me of the passing away of Lottie B. Caldwell, Mom, as I had come to know her. I immediately arranged a flight to San Francisco. It was a very sad journey, but one I felt compelled to make because, during her lifetime, she had made so many journeys to be with me. Somehow she had always, without any exception, managed to be with me during some of the most important moments of my life. It just seemed that I could not do without her presence.

James and Lottie Caldwell

Jim Hill visiting Lottie Caldwell in 1990 at her home in San Francisco.

Lottie's husband, James Caldwell, had passed away in 1968, just two weeks following our relocation to Fort Lauderdale. I attended his funeral and had visited Mom Caldwell only once since October 1990. Now came my last opportunity to be with her, even though it was too late to have been of comfort to Mom when she obviously needed it most. As a young boy, it was my grandparents, Garfield and Marie Chambers, who were always there to support me when Mother was not available. I never forgot that. As an adult, my adopted godparents, James and Lottie Caldwell, stepped up to fulfill this role as only they knew how. I often wondered if godparents were sent by God, but the Caldwells provided me with the answer.

Evelyn Ray Rogers, Lottie Caldwell's niece, had been with her aunt during the final few days of her life. Upon my arrival in San Francisco, Evelyn informed me of the many ordeals her aunt had gone through before her death. She assured me that my presence on this occasion would have pleased Lottie more than anyone would know. I had arrived in San Francisco as early as I could to be of assistance to members of the Ray family. Preparing a special dinner for the Ray family and friends was the only gesture I could think of that the Caldwells would have wanted me to make. Hosting such occasions was always their favorite way of entertaining their family and friends. It was my only way of telling Mom that "I didn't forget."

Jim Hill dining with the Ray family. (l to r) Mary Westbrook, Evelyn Rogers, Alma Ray, Jim Hill, Jeanette Goins, and Vivian James.

Mrs. Caldwell was eulogized on May 2, 1997, at the Third Baptist Church, her home church for over forty years. Following the reading of her obituary, I felt a strong urge to speak. There was a message about this incredible Christian woman that I was afraid might otherwise go untold. My testimony was about the great love and consideration she and James always had for me. I gave the following account:

By their own choice, I became one of Lottie and James Caldwell's adopted godsons. I had the blessing of living in their home, loving, and worshiping with them for four of the most critical years of my life. Although I moved away from them in 1958 to serve in the United

States Air Force and have remained away for the past thirty-nine years while chasing my life's dream, I have always remained with the Caldwells in spirit. During my life, I was fortunate to have served four years in the air force, at Ellsworth, South Dakota. I have been fortunate to attend Howard University in Washington, D.C., to complete my undergraduate education. I have been fortunate to direct Boys Clubs of America in Newark, New Jersey; the state of New York; and Fort Lauderdale, Florida. I have been fortunate to help manage the City of Fort Lauderdale for the past twenty-nine years while raising my three children. In the end, one could say that I had been trying all these years to earn my way back home. I wanted to be near my own mother and the Caldwells someday and to try to pay back the great debt I will always owe them. It is what they did for me that has enabled me to stand so tall and proud before you today.

Looking back, in retrospect, I now realize that meeting the Caldwells, these two incredible people, was no coincidence. It had to have been God's way of working things out for me back then. My grandparents, Garfield and Marie Chambers, had always told me how the Lord opens doors that we are unable to see. Well, the picture is clear to me now.

As a poor, young boy growing up in the rural community of Austin, I needed and received a lot of attention and support from my parents, relatives, neighbors, and friends. One month before graduating from high school in 1955, my aunt, Mary Westbrook, made a surprise fact-finding visit to my school in Austin to inquire about my high school records and about my plans to attend college. Through the private inquiries she made with my teachers, football coach, and parents, she found out that although my academic and athletic accomplishments were well above that required to attend the University of

Mrs. Lottie Caldwell (third row center) attending Eva and Jim's wedding in Austin, Texas, in 1966.

Texas, I would not be financially able to attend any college at the time. Neither my parents nor I could afford my education. Learning all this, Aunt Mary convinced my parents to allow me to come to California to attend junior college where I could perhaps work and earn my own way. So I left home at seventeen years of age by Greyhound Bus with only $28 in my pocket. Aunt Mary arranged a job for me in only five days after my arrival, and on the tenth day she took me over to meet Lottie and James Caldwell, her long-time friends who had become like family over the years. They gave me a room in their home in which to live, and we became inseparable thereafter.

The Caldwells had journeyed with me through all the important seasons of my life. They saw me off to the military. They stood with me to receive my first degree at Howard University and were present to hear me repeat my wedding vows to my wife Eva. Mom traveled to Fort Lauderdale on several occasions to honor my family and me as a special guest in our home. We celebrated to the highest in no less than grand style. We visited Mt. Olive Baptist Church together, and after hearing Reverend Weaver preach Mom fell in love with him just as she had always done with outstanding spiritual leaders. She liked her preachers!

I learned so many valuable lessons about life and living from the Caldwells. Like my parents and grandparents, these adopted godparents, through their daily living examples, had taught me the real meaning of loving, sharing, loyalty, and devotion to family and the church. Therefore, in conclusion, I would like to acknowledge and to thank God for Mr. and Mrs. Caldwell and for Aunt Mary for the major role she played in bringing us together. I believe that Evelyn Rogers and other relatives and friends who were fortunate to have been near Mom during those last few winter days of her life might tend to remember the way Lottie died, but I will remember her best for the way she lived. ✄

25

The Community of St. John

(The Role of Pioneer Parents)

With most of the family grown up and starting their own families, Marie and Garfield moved in and about the community of St. John meeting their new neighbors, seeking a new church affiliation, and volunteering their support of the neighborhood school, Fiskville Elementary. Garfield had been a long-time admirer of the Reverend A. K. Black, from whom he had purchased his two lots. He had labeled Reverend Black as a wise businessman, a man of vision, one you could trust. He would always urge Negroes to purchase as much land as possible, individually, or as groups, because there was power to be gained in ownership.

Rev. A. K. Black

Were it not for the courageous and visionary powers displayed by the late Reverend A. K. Black, Dr. L. L. Campbell, Rev. Ike Robinson, and Amos Clark and his son George, the St. John's Regular Baptist Association, as we know it today, might never have been conceived and developed and may not have continued to grow to become one of the largest organizations of its kind in the United States.

Dr. L. L. Campbell

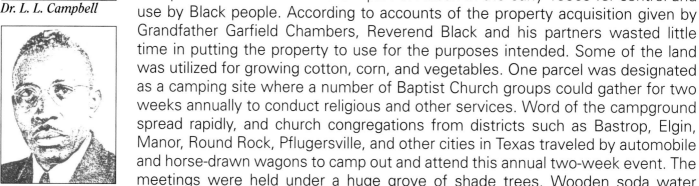

Rev. Ike Robinson

Bonded by the philosophy that there is strength in unity and power in the group, these pioneer forerunners of the community pooled their knowledge and financial resources together to buy and to develop hundreds of acres of prime un-incorporated land in the northern part of Austin in the early 1930s for control and use by Black people. According to accounts of the property acquisition given by Grandfather Garfield Chambers, Reverend Black and his partners wasted little time in putting the property to use for the purposes intended. Some of the land was utilized for growing cotton, corn, and vegetables. One parcel was designated as a camping site where a number of Baptist Church groups could gather for two weeks annually to conduct religious and other services. Word of the campground spread rapidly, and church congregations from districts such as Bastrop, Elgin, Manor, Round Rock, Pflugerville, and other cities in Texas traveled by automobile and horse-drawn wagons to camp out and attend this annual two-week event. The meetings were held under a huge grove of shade trees. Wooden soda water crates were used for seating unless you brought your own personal stool from home. Most members attending from other districts would pitch tents on the ground to live in for the two weeks of the meeting. Food was prepared in a variety of ways: by open fire on the ground, portable gas stoves, barbecue grills, and, occasionally, by electric warmers. From this humble beginning, the St. John's Regular Baptist Association became more organized in structure and has grown to what it is today.

Based on the chronological development of the St. John's Association property written by Audrey Batement in the June 17, 1977, edition of *The Austin American-Statesman* newspaper, three hundred three acres of land were purchased in the north area of Austin in 1894 by the St. John's Regular Baptist Association. Eleven years later (1911), the St. John's Home for Negro Orphans was built. The depression of the 1930s, however, brought financial problems to the organization, which forced the closing of the orphanage in 1942. The old buildings remained vacant for fourteen years before being destroyed by fire in 1951; that same year the property was sold. The fire which destroyed the orphanage in 1951 had erased one of St. John's oldest and most significant historical landmarks.

In October 2004, Jim Hill met with Austin Councilman Danny Thomas, the Community Development staff, and members of the St. John's Neighborhood Association to discuss the historical significance of the St. John's Orphanage in relation to the community at large. The purpose of the discussion was to obtain their endorsement for an upcoming project which reflected back to the memories of the orphanage.

Summer encampments brought thousands to St. John's Orphanage grounds

James Hill (bottom right) addressing the Austin Councilman Danny Thomas, Community Development Staff, and members of the St. John's Neighborhood Association at the Association meeting held October 5, 2004.

Another parcel of land was designated as a site for an orphanage and a school, where homeless individuals and families could reside or children without parents could stay and attend school until adopted. Both buildings were three stories high with a tall iron fire escape slide attached to the exterior side of each building. As children about twelve years of age, we would often go there to climb up and slide down the slides. We had enjoyed some of the most fun days of our lives playing around and running through the many dark and vacant rooms as the buildings started to deteriorate with age. Unaware of the possible danger the buildings presented, we children continued to play in them until they were condemned by the county. The buildings were left standing and unoccupied for a number of years until finally destroyed by fire. Smoke and flames from the old buildings formed a thick blanket of dark clouds over all of St. John, as if to say, "The end of progress of this community was near."

The largest and remaining parcels of land purchased by Reverend Black and his group were earmarked to be sold to Black families for building their own homes, schools, churches, and businesses. In a way, this land became the "promised land" for many Black families, including the Chambers family. Lots were sold for the moderate price of $50 per lot. People living on farms as sharecroppers became knowledgeable of these land sales while attending the St. John Association, and many decided to buy without delay. Reverend Black preached about land ownership almost every Sunday. "There is power in owning your own land," he said, "and one must always remember to cast a vote in every public election. It's your duty, my sisters and brothers." I remember that it was on one such morning that Reverend Black shared with the congregation his final vision of the future for St. John. His vision was that someday the community would have its own hospital with comfortable beds and large blue operating rooms for its patients. Black doctors and Black nurses graduating from medical schools, owned and operated by Blacks, coming to serve patients in their own communities were the essence of his dream. He then paused in silence and began to shed tears. Reverend Black would often weep following some of his speeches. I wondered if his weeping was his way of expressing his sadness for the bitterness some Caucasians displayed toward him because he would not yield to their greed for the land he owned that was being sold to Blacks in St. John.

As his vision began to become a reality, Reverend Black and his group were beginning to be pressured by major developers to sell this valuable land in St. John. Ultimately, with time, over half the acreage of St. John was sold to make way for the city to expand its businesses and commercial boundaries northward. A huge shopping center (Highland Mall) with tons of asphalt now covers the rich and fertile soil that produced our crops of cotton and corn and served as habitats for small game we hunted as kids. Reverend Black died shortly after the land was sold.

Although completely surrounded by numerous retail and commercial giants, the old St. John residential community still stands. What remains of Big Momma and Big Poppa's old home place where I grew up is only the concrete front porch with iron rails they would hold to get up and down. This was the price they paid for progress. It happens throughout America. It had finally happened in St. John. Marie and Garfield Chambers experienced it. They knew that it was all for real. Running through time, they were unaware that their foresight, courage, and brotherhood would someday win for them the victory of achieving their goals. Rev. A. K. Black, L. L. Campbell, Ike Robinson, Amos Clark and his son Rev. George Clark are all names that rest in history, along with the memories of all of us who lived in St. John.

Rev. A. K. Black later founded Blacks Memorial Baptist Church, and with the assistance of several dedicated family group members the church grew from a wooden storefront facility where wooden soda water bottle crates were utilized for chairs to a rock building facility in just a few years. Garfield and Marie Chambers were among the pioneer church members who helped develop the church. Mr. and Mrs. Sam Harris were another pioneer couple who worked hand in hand with Reverend Black to develop Blacks Memorial Baptist Church. Garfield and Sam Harris became heads of the Deacon and Trustee Boards of the church where they served for over thirty years before passing away. The church had become the center of their lives.

Other pioneer members of this St. John landmark church community included Mr. and Mrs. Madison Brown, Mrs. Sarah Fennell, Mr. and Mrs. Elsie Grey, Mr. and Mrs. Hugh Green, Mrs. Bedford, and Mrs. Salina Collins and husband. There were many others, but I was too young to recall all of them. I grew up in Blacks Memorial Baptist Church, was baptized at ten years of age by Reverend Black, and looked forward to visiting this church with my mother, Ethel Hill, each summer while vacationing in Austin. Every time I go inside the church, or even pass by it, I can feel the presence of Marie and Garfield and all the pioneers. In my mind, I hear them praying and singing those "Old 100 Hymns" they often sang during the devotional part of the service, which, as a child, I always thought was too long.

Samuel Harris

Sarah Fennell (l) and Marie Chambers (r) in their late 80s.

Pioneer community parents of St. John did much more than develop the churches. As extended family role models, they provided leadership, guidance, and counseling for all young people who were in need. Opportunities for emotional and physical development were provided by Mr. Louis Roberts, Little League baseball coach for the neighborhood team. Mr. and Mrs. James Dean were den mother and father for the Cub Scout and Boy Scout troops. Adel and Junious Scott managed the Brownies and Girl Scouts and chaperoned almost every special event planned by Fiskville School. Additionally, Mrs. Beatrice Dean, "Aunt Tiny," as we called her, was coordinator of the Fiskville School lunch program and was responsible for ensuring a balanced lunch diet for all students. Marie Chambers and other parents volunteered to assist with the lunch program as often as they could.

Junious Scott and Mr. Jackson

Mr. and Mrs. Louis Roberts Sr.

Mr. Turner and Mr. Brown were asked one day by Principal Phillips to perform one of the most unusual volunteer jobs. These fathers were asked to build a fire to smoke student Ernest Wright, who had somehow been sprayed by a pole cat one night. Smoke will diffuse skunk odor better than anything else I know. Annual school Easter egg hunts, 4-H field trips, basketball and softball games, and drama productions were a list of activities sponsored by the community school which always involved the parents. Teachers such as Mrs. Della Phillips, Ms. Norma Dodson, Ms. Upshaw, Ms. Cooper, Ms. Strong, and Mr. Battle were worshiped by the students and the parents, and they deserved every bit of it.

Adel Scott

Law enforcement was almost never required in the community of St. John prior to 1950. Whenever it was needed, however, Sheriff Tom Plummer would always respond on time. Just to hear Tom Plummer's name struck fear in every child. Sheriff Plummer would never jail a youth; he would punish the child and then take him home to the parents. This usually corrected the problem.

Students who grew up in St. John, attended Fiskville School, and who were subjected to the Pioneer Community Parent System usually graduated from high school, went on to college, and have grown up to become outstanding citizens of the communities where they reside. Prior to the early 1950s, families of the St. John community had only three movie theaters, or "picture shows," as we called them in those days, that we could attend to see our favorite Western movies, reruns of boxing championship fights, or adventure series, such as *Batman & Robin*, *Superman*, or the *Adventures of Sir Galahad*. The Harlem Theater, located in East Austin, or the Carver Theater, located on Sixth Street in downtown Austin, were the only theaters built at the time for Blacks. Colored people, however, were permitted to attend the Ritz, Yank, and Paramount Theaters in Austin. But they had to sit in a special section, either upstairs or downstairs. They could attend only on certain occasions or for a particular showing. I saw the movie *Carmen Jones* at the Paramount in 1951. That was my first visit to a Whites-only theater as a child, but, to me, it felt no different from other theaters where I had gone. Black parents never feared for our welfare or safety while we were there, which was a reflection of the mature, high level of racial tolerance for which Austin residents always have been known.

Thanks to the initiative of Mr. Willie Williams and the other members of this early St. John pioneering family, residents of St. John no longer had to travel twelve miles to the city to enjoy a movie. Members of the Williams family were skilled construction and mason contractors who had built a number of houses and other buildings throughout St. John and the Greater Austin area. The Williamses built, owned, and operated the first movie theater and a small cafe in the St. John community during the early 1950s. Pioneer parents Mrs. Collins and Mrs. Sneed chaperoned many young people of the community to and from the movies every Saturday night and from evening church services on Sundays. As the St. John community grew and progressed, this first old movie building they had built was renovated for use as the community social services center. My mother attended meetings at the facility on a monthly basis where the Williamses' old home place still stands vacant next to the center as a memorial landmark to remind us of how things were and what we must now do to protect and preserve our heritage.

Because of people like the Chambers and their contemporaries, the St. John community became a very close-knit neighborhood where every family knew each other, even as late as the early 1950s when St. John became incorporated into the city of Austin. In this neighborhood, every parent, by mutual consent, was permitted to discipline any child who was observed misbehaving. Whenever such discipline became necessary, the parent who administered the discipline would report the incident to the child's own parents that same day, and in most cases the child received additional discipline from his own parents. Social interaction such as described above resulted in the development of a rather impressive list of neighborhood mothers and fathers.

Neighborhood pioneer mothers and fathers included the earliest settlers and developers of the St. John community who provided the leadership, support, and stability of the school, the church, and the social structure of the neighborhood. Marie and Garfield Chambers were part of this distinguished pioneer community parent group who took interest in every child in the neighborhood. They were trusted and highly respected by every child and adult who knew them. People who settled in St. John seldom asked each other where they had moved from or why they had decided to locate in this neighborhood. My guess, however, is that most of the people had moved to St. John from some rural community in Texas, as the Chambers had. Love of family, church, school, and neighbors was a common value they all shared. All youth in the neighborhood were encouraged to learn about work at an early age. Summer vacation for many youth of St. John consisted of going to pick cotton with their parents who were on vacation from their regular jobs. This sometimes consisted of camping out on the farm for a week, or months at a time, before returning home for school. We considered these outings to be both recreation and work. This was how the family paid for school clothes for the year while spending some quality time together.

Several youngsters managed to land some rather impressive part-time jobs after school. Robert Turner, for example, had the first newspaper route. The Fennell brothers did carpentry work with their father. I did lawn work and built ranch fences with my stepfather on weekends. Many evenings during the school year I would spade the Taylors' flower beds when I could not get a marble game going. Frank Shaw learned to repair cars by assisting his father and grew up to become one of Austin's top professional mechanics. Willie "Skip" Jones, the first St. John student to play varsity football for Anderson High School, earned enough money from odd jobs to buy a car. Skip was a role model for all younger guys in St. John, a real gentleman with a great personality. The Hendricks brothers, Clarence and Jimmy,

Turner Brothers (l to r): Odell, Herman, Leward, and Robert.

were model athletes of Fiskville School. They knew the meaning of sportsmanship, community pride, and moral values. They became leaders of College Heights Baptist Church.

St. John is a community with tradition. In the state of Texas, Blacks celebrate the 19th of June, or "Juneteenth," annually. This was the day when Texas received word that President Abraham Lincoln had signed the Emancipation Proclamation, freeing all slaves in the United States. The St. John neighborhood celebrated this occasion in a very big way. All the churches in St. John united to form a special committee to plan and to coordinate a program for the occasion. The churches donated all the funds for the celebration to make sure that there was enough of everything for everybody. It was all free! Garfield Chambers, Sam Harris, and Deacon Board representatives from each church in the neighborhood went out and purchased live cows, calves, goats, sheep, and chickens which they stayed up all night slaughtering and barbecuing for the big feast. Pioneer parents and missionary societies of the churches prepared the cakes, pies, vegetables, and bread for dinner. This big event was always staged in Black's Bottom Park, a neighborhood park also owned by Reverend Black. The young people had fun swimming in the bottomless dam where almost every boy in St. John first learned to swim. I learned how to swim by being thrown into the dam, with all my clothes on, by the older boys.

Baseball and other games were played while dinner was being served. Everyone at the picnic wore brightly colored clothing on this day and drank red Kool-Aid until our stomachs could hold no more. Church service was the order of the evening, and political speeches followed. Celebrations such as this seem to have given meaningful significance to the Emancipation Proclamation. But, as the 1960s approached, the Juneteenth celebration had begun to lose its significance and was, ultimately, discontinued in St. John in favor of the Fourth of July. The early 1980s, however, beckoned the return of the significance of the Juneteenth, not only in Texas, but in other states as well.

Prior to 1948, all homes in St. John utilized wood and kerosene fuel for cooking and lighting. Radios were all battery-operated and were the primary source of entertainment and world news. Innovations on a very small scale began to occur around 1949, when Arthur Taylor and Mr. E.J. combined to install a three-mile electric power line from the nearest city power line directly to their homes, which had been wired by Seallen Chambers, to accommodate this source of power. These were the first two homes in St. John to be powered by electricity. The Clifford and Rose Chambers family was the first to own a television in the neighborhood. The advent of electricity and television signaled that the

Arthur Taylor

end of the rural, suburban lifestyle we had been accustomed to for so many years was about to change, and change it did.

Rev. A. K. Black's vision of the 1930s, that Negroes could create a community in St. John which could function autonomously from Whites, had become a reality. Negroes had bought up the land, established churches, grocery stores, dry cleaners, carpentry and electronics services, as well as barber and beauty shops. The population of St. John had peaked and was beginning to take on the atmosphere of an urban community. The most convincing evidence of Reverend Black's dream, however, was the tremendous upsurge in school enrollment and retention on all academic levels, particularly on the college level, that Blacks were experiencing in Austin and throughout the United States at the time. Pioneer parents, including Marie and Garfield, were becoming increasingly concerned about the possibility of Austin expanding its northern corporate boundaries to include the St. John settlement. By the late 1950s, many young families that had grown up in St. John began to relocate to the east-side neighborhoods of Austin, three years before St. John was ultimately incorporated by the city of Austin, around 1958.

Clifford Chambers

Urbanization impacted St. John in numerous ways. First, every home had to be upgraded to conform to city codes. Water and sewer services, street lighting, paved streets, and weekly garbage collection were all now mandated by government. No farm animals were allowed to be housed in the neighborhood. Second, in 1954, the U.S. Supreme Court decision signaling the end of segregation in public schools raised immediate speculation that Fiskville School was nearing its final years of operation. By order of the court decision, four years later, in 1958, Fiskville School was history. It was closed, demolished, and later replaced by St. John Elementary School, located only a short distance from where the old school stood. The latter also was closed in 1971 in the name of integration.

Garfield and Marie Chambers, two people who had always been in favor of improved education for their children and grandchildren, were greatly saddened by the demise of Fiskville School. Most pioneer parents felt this to be the greatest loss the community had ever encountered. The social and historical significance of this school was realized by everyone more than ever because busing children from St. John to other schools in Austin was a visible symbol to remind them of how things in the community used to be.

Fiskville School

No longer able to walk just a few short blocks to see his grandchildren perform in school activities, Garfield became mildly depressed by all the changes he observed taking place in the community he helped build. Following a brief illness, he died. Away starting my professional career with the Boys Clubs in New Jersey, I had no funds to travel to his funeral. Marie, his devoted wife for over sixty-three years, simply wore out physically and at 103 years of age passed away, falling short of her mother Lilia's lifespan by seven years. Regretfully, neither of my grandparents were alive to witness the building and opening of the ultramodern Pickel Elementary School facility presently serving the St. John neighborhood since September 2002. Seeing this new school, however, makes me real proud to report that the old St. John community is still alive and well today.

The Chambers house was demolished in 1989 to accommodate the widening of Highway I-35. The remaining portion of their commercially zoned lots was sold on January 25, 2002, to accommodate further commercial development of the area. Not a day passes that I do not think about this home that my grandparents had built and had shared with all of us. I also think of the community parents of St. John and the special interest they always took in me. I just hope that someday I can go back to see my old friends, shake their hands, and thank them for helping me to remember who I am, where I came from, and how I got to be where I am today.

I graduated from Anderson High School and departed from St. John to attend college in San Francisco, California, in August of 1955. I never returned to live in St. John, but my roots will always remain there. Although the name *St. John* has been more commonly referred to by many as "St. Johns," it will always be denoted as the same for me. It is my home. ⚎

Pioneer Parents of St. John Community…Never to be Forgotten

Mr. and Mrs. George Washington

Mr. Shaw with granddaughter

Mrs. Shaw and son

Susie Terry and grandchildren

Sarah Fennell

Mrs. Pearl Fletcher

Mrs. Gertrude Taylor

Mr. Jim Fletcher

Emanuel E. Hill, Jr.

Pioneer Parents of St. John Community...Never to be Forgotten

Mrs. Alberta Brown

Mr. Laurence Brown

Mr. and Mrs. Junious Scott and Mary Pleasant

Mr. Pleasant and Mamie

Ms. Emma Filmore and mother

Susie A. Warren Harris

Marie and Garfield Chambers

Mrs. William Turner

Mr. Jack Scott

Mrs. Viola Scott and granddaughters

Pioneer Parents of St. John Community…Never to be Forgotten

Mr. and Mrs. Joe Ford

Mrs. Salinas Collins

Mr. and Mrs. Jack Alexander

Mr. and Mrs. Jackson

Mr. Albert Powell

Mr. Ambrus Cyphers and wife

(l to r) Bennie Williams, his son, grandson, and great-grandson.

James Dean attending civic meeting

Mr. and Mrs. James Dean with family and relatives

Louise Scott, Adel Scott, and Ruby Scott

Mrs. Vida Cyphers

26

A Surprise Return to Home Base

(St. John)

Mother's aging condition had become an increasing matter of concern to me, and the urge to come home had grown more demanding with each passing day. It is a bad thing for elderly people, like Mother, to have to live in fear. My first, and most important, purpose for making this sudden, unexpected journey home on October 6, 1995, was to try to reduce the fear she had been quietly experiencing since my last visit home, almost a year ago.

The Chambers old home demolished, but steps and porch are still there.

To reminisce about the childhood years I spent growing up here, I had the occasion to visit this incredible old neighborhood of north Austin. Under a perfect blue Texas fall day sky, I traveled both streets of old St. John, first up Blackson Avenue and then down Delmont, the only two main streets the neighborhood has.

The V. K. Black's general store and residence, which were the first buildings located on Blackson Avenue fifty years ago, had long been razed to accommodate the building of Highway I-35. All that was left of the home place which Garfield and Marie Chambers had built fifty-six years ago was the front porch with the handrail that was later installed with U.S. government funds to assist them going in and out of their home during their golden years. The property was sold and redeveloped by the year 2003.

Manny Hill house

The Emanuel Hill home was located across the street directly in front of the Chambers home. I will always remember the Hill house because the front porch of this house was the scene of the only fight I have ever had with a girl.

At eleven years of age, I was sitting leisurely on my grandparents' front porch one hot summer morning talking to my cousin Jean Allen. Charlesa Jackson, a neighbor, was at the Hill house visiting Mary Emma Hill on the front porch of their home. Charlesa Jackson was a couple of years older than I and sometimes enjoyed teasing and picking on the younger boys in the neighborhood, such as me. On this particular morning, Charlesa was meddling and saying funny things about me that I could not exactly hear. I became extremely angry and went over to the Hill front porch where we fought. During our fight, Charlesa got me down and was whipping me real good. Had not Grandmother Chambers come over to stop the fight, Charlesa might have shaken me up very badly. Charlesa and I were good friends all of our lives, but the fight between us was always remembered by the kids of St. John. It was remembered as the fight I started with a girl who beat me. My grandparents never approved of me fighting boys or girls, so I never fought again.

Beatrice Dean's home place

The Reed home place, located at the west end of Blackson Avenue, has been replaced by a two-story residence, which is the only one of its kind to be built in this neighborhood.

The Reed Family Home Place

My first visit on Delmont Avenue was to Mrs. Beatrice Dean's home where she resided alone at the time. My brief visit with "Aunt Tiny" was as warm and exciting as it was the last time I saw her forty years ago. Her son and her husband had both passed away.

I observed the Turner, Brown, and Bedford home places as I rushed to the beginning of Delmont Avenue, where Fiskville Elementary School once stood. The site of Fiskville remained undeveloped from 1958 when it was demolished until its redevelopment in 1997. Highway I-35 consists of eight traffic lanes. The western four lanes of this highway were once the outdoor dirt basketball court. Here we learned to play organized, competitive basketball as the "Fiskville Maroons." It was also the school's playground. The first activities of every new school year consisted of the students pulling weeds and cutting grass.

Fiskville School; the site was still vacant in 1995.

Finally, before crossing the highway to return to my car, I allowed my eyes to follow the traffic as it swiftly moved southward up the hill to St. John Avenue, where a large Home Depot store was recently built.

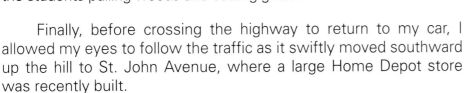

New Home Depot in St. John

While en route to my own old home place, I stopped briefly at the corner of Blackson Avenue and Providence Street to admire the ball field and park that have been constructed only two blocks from my home. Children who grew up with me would have enjoyed having such a beautiful facility in the neighborhood, but we learned to enjoy what we had.

Thelma Williams

The excitement of being home on this unexpected visit continued to mount when I called on the Bennie Williams home to pick up a photograph of this outstanding community pioneer. During my brief visit with the

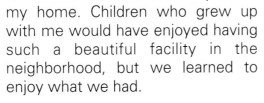

Ball field near my old home in St. John

Williamses, I had the pleasant opportunity of meeting one of St. John's own young stars, Ms. Thelma Williams, the author of several published books and numerous other literary and art forms. Thelma, like me, is a native of Austin. She also grew up in St. John, as did I and the gifted and soulful musician-singer-songwriter W. C. Clark. Today, although strapped by the awesome demands imposed upon them by their professional careers, Thelma and W. C. are both committed to looking at the whole picture of Austin and St. John.

W. C. Clark

Through this concerted commitment by all of us, we hope our efforts are serving to motivate and to encourage a strong work ethic that will empower youths everywhere in America to pursue higher learning, professional careers, and entrepreneurship. Perhaps, by our own examples, we will help save young men and women from the "street life" by confirming the fact that there are numerous other achievable options available to them in spite of prevailing socioeconomic conditions.

Corbie and daughter Jasmin in Great-grandmother Hill's yard.

Having learned of this book that I was in the process of writing, Thelma graciously allowed me to include the poem she had written about our own community, St. Johns, now location of the St. John Association Camping Facility, purchased and built with funds from the sale of the three hundred acres of the orphanage land which previously had been

Ethel (center) sits, overwhelmed at the party

St. Johns

My background tells the story of never having enough.
Sitting on my porch, I wondered why this area had it so tough.

Urban renewal sold us a dream of owning our own land.
By purchasing property, we could become our own man.

Happily moving from the country, no more picking cotton and such,
But moving was just the beginning – we still had it rough.

Our property had no restrictions like that of the whiteman,
So we had no water or electricity and no money to take a stand.

I asked my grandfather once why "nigger" was my name?
He would gently say daughter, ignorance is to blame.

Some people think they're better, coming from a different place,
Some people think they're better, coming from a different race.

We are all God's children, in this land of the free,
With faith, patience and kindness, things will be what they should be.

Changes have been made, and my grandfather has gone away,
The city brought forth water, and light made darkness like day.

They paved all the streets, me and many schoolmates left town,
Taxes took many houses, and building broke new ground.

Whites and Blacks stopped fighting long enough to mix the schools,
Black children had problems learning the white's Golden rules.

Thirty years have passed and St. Johns is the place,
Where I've decided to share my talents, making this my home base.

by Thelma Williams

purchased from the Association by Herman Brown in 1956. Thelma's description of the community and its people, as described in her poem, is true. I am thrilled just to know Thelma and concur with her deep appreciation of the kind of neighborhood St. John once was.

As the time drew near for my departure from St. John, I kept thinking of some appropriate ways to commemorate this most unexpected visit home. My niece Diane and I threw an impromptu party the night before I was to return to Florida. Mother was all dressed up to receive her guests. She was excited to have her family and relatives drop in for this enjoyable evening. My grandniece Corbie brought her daughter Jasmin, my great-grandniece, to meet me for the first time.

This visit was such a delight, and I came away looking forward to the next get-together to spend some quality time with both old and young friends. One visit I particularly look forward to is the cordial invitation extended to me by a St. John's Junior League Baseball playmate of mine, the Reverend Dr. George V. Clark, moderator of St. John's Regular Baptist Association, to visit the annual camp meeting for the first time in fifty years. ✠

27

The Family in Perspective

(With Malice Toward None)

During the early 1900s, when our grandparents were approaching their young adulthood, most Americans looked upon a "proper" family life with a set of beliefs that a *family* was comprised of a married couple and their minor children living together in the same residence. The father, as head of the household, was expected to earn the family's income single-handedly and to determine the family's residence. His surname became that of his wife and children. The mother's primary role was to serve as her husband's companion and helper, staying home and devoting herself full-time to the tasks of rearing the children and homemaking.

These grandparents had exclusive responsibilities for the care of their children until the children reached school age. The Chambers couple were free to discipline their children as they saw fit. As members of a society which fostered a strong family-oriented culture, one in which the family was the fundamental unit, they totally conformed to the foregoing definition of a family.

That society they once understood so well had shifted from a society in which the individuals were nothing apart from their family identity to a society in which the individual was now of central importance. However, as the 1950s and 1960s approached, Garfield and Marie had begun to experience these great changes that had occurred in the nature and the form of the family as we know it today, even including their own family. However, as sudden and far-reaching as these changes were, Garfield and Marie were recognizing, for the first time, that these changes did not begin in the last two decades, or even the last half-century; they had taken place over the past three hundred years.

The most distinguishing characteristic of American family life since 1960 has been the increasing diversity in family arrangements. Today, young people marry much later, and more elderly people live by themselves. The number of stepfamilies has increased, and now more than one tenth of this nation's children live with one stepparent and one natural parent. Higher divorce rates, coupled with an increase in the number of children born to single women, have led to more families being headed by females. According to historian Steven Mintz and anthropologist Susan Kellogg, approximately 44 percent of Black families nowadays in America are headed by females. Marie and Garfield had become very concerned about the impact these changes might have on the members of our family in future years.

Marshall Toliver and wife exchanging wedding vows.

The last time I saw Grandfather Garfield alive was in 1958 when I came home after completing my basic training for the United States Air Force in San Antonio. He was concerned at the time about the possibility of another world war and the situation developing in Berlin. Admiring my appearance in the Class "A" Air Force uniform, Grandfather stood on his front porch and waved to me, the grandson he had helped raise, the young man whom he had watched grow up, who was leaving the St. John community in search of a future in some other place in the world. Some of the many changes which he observed affecting other families had already begun to affect some members of his own, especially the younger generation.

Garfield and Marie often discussed the impact of divorce on the family. They recognized through their own observations how effective stepparents can be if carefully selected. My stepfather, Mr. E.J. Hill, and Uncles Olen Toliver and Seallen Chambers were of the finest examples. They recognized that teenage pregnancy, drug abuse, and alcoholism were among some of the social ills that were affecting young people more than ever before. They were hopeful and prayed daily that their grandchildren, great-grandchildren, great-great-grandchildren, and even their own adult sons and daughters, would stay free of these life hazards. Would the good example they had tried to set all

Chambers great-grandson, Jim Hill II, sworn in as Second Lieutenant in the U.S. Army.

their lives as Christian workers in the church, parents, good neighbors, good providers for their family, and law-abiding citizens be enough to influence their younger generations in the years to come? was a question they often asked themselves. Garfield passed away on June 24, 1966, twenty-one years prior to his wife Marie's death on July 29, 1987, and was denied the pleasure of seeing many of his offspring grow into adulthood. But Marie Chambers lived to celebrate her 103d birthday and to witness the births of her thirty-fifth and thirty-sixth grandchildren, Dwight and Nell Chambers.

Born children of former slaves and having been exposed to prejudice and the old Jim Crow southern way of life, Big Momma and Big Poppa harbored no hatred or bitterness toward anyone. They were proud to be Texans and never considered Texas as being a southern state. This feeling was shared by most people who lived in Texas, including me. Just why we felt this way was somewhat of a puzzle to me until I finally did some research on the issue.

In his book *An Empire for Slavery: The Peculiar Institution in Texas, 1821-1865*, Ralph B. Campbell reported that, historically:

> there is a widespread misconception, particularly in Texas, that somehow the institution of Negro slavery was not very important in the Lone Star state. This is not really surprising in that many historians, writers, and creators of popular culture have preferred to see Texas as essentially western rather than southern. . . . So long as Texas is not seen as a southern state, its people do not have to face the great moral evil of slavery and the bitter heritage of black-white relations that followed the defeat of the Confederacy in 1865 (p. 1).

This popular misconception that my grandparents and I had of Texas perhaps best explains why we never exhibited the bitterness toward Whites that some Blacks often exhibited in other areas of the South where slavery was more prevalent. The Reese and the Chambers families have successfully coexisted with Whites and Hispanics for over a century. Several interracial marriages have expanded the multiethnic base of this family by a considerable degree. There is some evidence that this base could expand in the latter generations.

Ralph Taylor holding his niece Tamara while congratulating brother Lester Taylor and wife on their new addition to the family.

However, the facts must never be forgotten.

> Antebellum Texas considered slavery vital to their future. The first settlers in Stephen F. Austin's colony brought slaves, and Austin himself, although not particularly devoted to slavery . . ., concluded by 1933 that "Texas *must be* a slave country. Circumstances and unavoidable necessity compels it. It is the wish of the people there, and it is my duty to do all I can, prudently, in favor of it. I will do so" (Stephen F. Austin to Wiley Martin, May 30, 1833, as cited in Campbell, p. 3).

Charles DeMorse, Massachusetts-born editor of the Clarksville *Northern Standard* newspaper, wrote in 1859:

> "We care nothing for . . . slavery as an abstraction—but we desire the practicality; the increase of our productions; the increase of the comforts and wealth of the population; and if slavery, or slave labor, or Negro Apprentice labor ministers to this, why that is what we want" (Stephen F. Austin to Wiley Martin, May 30, 1833, as cited in Campbell, p. 3).

Recalling her conversation held with Great-grandmother Lilia Reese shortly before her death, Aunt Lillian Chambers asked Lilia what she remembered most about the Capitol State Building of Texas, located in Austin. Lilia replied, "The Capitol Building chills my spirit and makes me very angry even to this very day because it reminds me of the fact that my brother was whipped and died there during the construction of the building. As a slave, he was whipped to death by his overseer for getting too tired to carry the cement blocks for building the structure."

Given the above facts that our native home state of Texas is a southern state and did benefit from slave activities, the Chambers family has remained loyal to and proud of the Lone Star State. Just as a family's past does not determine its future, neither does a state's. Texas is a friendly state today, and Austin is a friendly city. It was people like our grandparents, Garfield and Marie, who helped make it that way. They lived and walked through their lives with open minds and willing hearts and with the one wish they treasured above all others, that we follow the examples they set.

28

Journey to Ghana, West Africa

(A Native's Return to His Homeland)

The research I had conducted earlier on the Reese-Chambers family had provided some general evidence to support my hypothesis that our family roots could originally have been anchored in Ghana, West Africa. Intrigued by the new information my wife Eva had brought back from her initial visit to Ghana in August 2000, I eagerly accepted the retirement gift offer from her to return to the country with her for a three-week vacation. The purpose of the trip would be for further study and research of this early assumption I had made regarding our family origin. Moreover, such a trip would serve to bring about a more dramatic closure to the many inquiries I had made over these past sixteen years regarding the history and the plight of the Reese-Chambers family.

Just the thought of making my first journey back to the original homeland of my people after all these years was thoroughly mindboggling. It meant that I would possibly be the first, and the only known member, of our family to return to Ghana since the horrifying capture and deportment of our earlier ancestors from their original native-free homelands. Through reading books such as *School Certificate: The History of West Africa*, written by K.B.C. Onwubiko, world-renowned African writer and scholar, I had learned that our ancestors were chained and then placed in cages aboard huge ships manufactured and operated by Dutch, French, English, and Portuguese explorers. The specific use of these ships was to transport Negro captives, as well as gold and ivory, from the west coast of Africa to the major slave markets throughout the world where slave labor was in great demand. It was from locations such as these that our early ancestors who survived the long, hard journey across the Atlantic Ocean were sold into slavery. Many of our African family members were separated and divided once again—never to see or to hear from each other ever again during their lifetimes.

As the date of my historic journey to Ghana drew near, thoughts surrounding the harrowing ordeal of my brethren before me continued to come and go from my mind at frequencies I had never previously experienced. Suddenly, Africa had taken on an entirely different meaning for me. A continent about which I had often heard so much was to no longer remain just a figment of my imagination. That dramatic landing of our Boeing 767 British Airways at Accra Airport in Ghana, West Africa, on the evening of September 5, 2001, assured me that Africa, at last, had become, for the first time, a reality in my life. The native had finally returned to his homeland.

Accompanied by the Reverend Martin Adu, a native of Ghana and a personal friend for many years, we entered the airport terminal to be greeted with the warmest of affection

Rev. Martin K. Adu, who provided family connection with Ghana during our visits in 2000 and 2001.

and love by members of the Adu family, who were joined by the Reverend Francis Boakey Towiah, a local priest. I am quite certain the first- and second-generation members of the Reese-Chambers family would recall every bit of detail about the people of West Africa, the many traditions and customs of the great Ashanti people of Ghana, both of which I am so eager to describe in this chapter. But for the six younger generations of our family, this information and account of my findings can only be viewed as an important educational experience that our family must continue to uncover whenever and wherever we can. Just as Great-great grandmother Miriah had to rely upon her parents and other elder relatives and countrymen for her education regarding the history and the plight of her ancestors, we must do likewise today.

While visiting Ghana, we were honored guests at the beautiful home of Mrs. Elizabeth Addai, the mother of the Reverend Martin Adu, and her family. The hospitality, friendship, and the extraordinary personal service received at the hands of this family during our visit was of the very highest caliber we had ever received from anyone we have ever visited for such an extended time. We were made to feel at home the moment we entered their house. The itinerary and the numerous preparations they had made for our visit were evidence that this family had made it a priority for Eva and me to learn, firsthand, as much as we could about the history and the people of West Africa. I especially wanted to meet and to interact with the people of Ghana and members of the great Ashanti Nation. Observations of their customs and their general way of life provided me with valuable clues and linkage that seemed to connect me with my family's past in a very simple and meaningful kind of way. Although a few of the customs I had observed were quite startling to me, most were very reassuring and culturally identifiable.

Our first adventure was a visit to the city of Kumasi, the second largest city in Ghana. We were given a guided tour of the Asantehene's Palace and Cultural Center by Mr. Osei Kwadwo, curator of Manhyia Palace Museum and author of a book titled *An Outline of Asante History*. Mr. Osei Kwadwo's vast knowledge of the rulers and kings of Ashanti enables him to articulate the life stories of the presidents and the kings of Ghana and chronicle its history with great clarity, style, and color. Following the tour, I purchased a copy of his book, which he graciously autographed for me. We also paused for a photograph. Every morning thereafter I would awake at 7 a.m. and spend the first two hours of each day reading about the rich history of my native homeland, the wars and the struggles it has undergone to become the country that it is today, and many other interesting facts that I had never known.

Our host family: (front row, l to r) Mr. Osbon, Architect; Mother Addai; Martin Adu; and Pius Twumasi; (back row, l to r) Peter Adu-Marfo; Eva and Jim Hill; Margaret Konama; and Augustine Amoako.

Mr. Osei Kwadwo (center) presenting copy of his book to me. Mrs. Sarah Nsiah-Asare, Father Martin, and Dan Poku accompanied me on the tour.

Geographically speaking, Ghana's sandy, unpaved roads and trails reminded me so much of those in Wilbarger County, Texas, where the members of the Chambers family spent the earlier years of their lives farming crops of corn, yams, and green vegetables, raising poultry and animals in much the same way as the Ashanti people do in Ghana today. The daily meals for most Ghanian families consist of yams, plantains, kontomire, banku, cassava, and a meat (i.e., goat, small fish, or beef). Guinea fowls or pheasants are most often eaten instead of chicken. Poultry farming is a popular small business in Ghana, where chickens are grown primarily for the production of eggs, which are marketed for extremely high prices.

A typical village unpaved roadway where children would transport water from the system to their homes throughout the village.

Chickens are sold for food only when they can no longer produce eggs. Young fryer chickens, such as what Americans consume on a daily basis, are considered to be a delicacy that is far too expensive for the average African family in Ghana to afford.

Many families in Ghana grow goats and sheep. These animals are allowed to feed and to graze freely throughout the neighborhood village wherever grass is to be found. Considered by most families to be assets, the goats and the sheep are not slaughtered for food but, instead, are allowed to grow and to multiply into sizable flocks, which are passed on to family members of the younger generation as a symbol of family wealth. Citrus, bananas, coconut, and cocoa plantations are numerous throughout the rain forest region of Ghana.

The role of males in Ashanti culture is primarily that of farming, construction, and governing the people of the village or the community where they reside. Based on personal observations I made, males do not assume or share any of the roles traditionally performed by females. My own grandfather and great-grandfather continued this same practice. But subsequent generations of our family find males performing almost every task traditionally performed by women, and we enjoy doing the tasks. In contrast, however, Ghanian females may often be seen performing a number of tasks traditionally performed by their counterparts.

Customs and traditions that I observed within African families were very interesting to me in that they served to remind me of the cultural teachings we still share in common, as well as those I must have forgotten because of a lack of practice. Females of the Ashanti culture assume the major role of housekeeping, as was the practice of Grandma Marie Chambers. In addition to this never-ending responsibility, West African women also collect the wood utilized for heating and cooking. Women work closely with the children of the family, who play a major role by transporting water from the community system to the house for cooking, washing the clothing, and bathing. Females and children are completely in charge of all household duties. Unlike most American families, Ghanaian children and adult females are often not permitted to sit around the table to consume their meals along with the special guests and adult males of the family.

Elderly persons are treated with great respect by other members of the family. They are generally exempted from performing any of the daily work chores except for those light tasks they voluntarily choose to perform. Mother Addai, senior female head of her household, for example, enjoyed sweeping the house and the yard around 5 a.m. daily, utilizing her very small handmade straw broom. Sitting outdoors observing and chatting with younger members of the family while they prepare the meals are common rituals for the elderly in Ghana.

Father Martin purchasing chickens from a nearby poultry farm for the dinner.

Having observed the customs and the roles of the Addai family members for two weeks, I thought it would be a fascinating experience for me to relieve the women and the young people of their responsibility of preparing and serving the meal for one day. For me to do so would be a complete break of the Ashanti tradition because men simply do not prepare meals for the family. I learned from this experience that preparing one family meal is a full day's job for anyone doing it. The menu I selected to prepare consisted of barbecued chicken, cabbage greens, okra gumbo, and corn bread. Collecting the food materials alone was a half day's work. I traveled two miles to the nearest poultry farm to purchase five live chickens, which I then had to kill and dress before cooking. Locating a small bit of pork fatback for seasoning the cabbage was another major task, as only one store in Kumasi sold pork. The Muslim population is quite large in Ghana; therefore, the demand for pork is low. Locating okra in Ghana during the month of September is no easy task either.

Jim making announcement that dinner is served

The meal I prepared for the Addai family and their associates was to serve a maximum of twenty-five people. When dinner was ready to be served, however, about three hundred guests from the village showed up. We tried to feed them all. The words *barbecued chicken* had somehow spread throughout the village that day, and the people responded accordingly. We literally served each person a spoonful of food. Preparing and sharing this small bit of food with all of these families left us with a most wonderful feeling beyond description. It was like the five loaves of bread and two fishes miracle performed by Jesus as recorded in the Bible. When dinner was concluded, I was given a warm round of applause by the guests. Father Martin said the closing prayer, and everyone returned to their homes. The women and the children of the Addai family resumed their normal duties, and I was ushered out of the kitchen. The cultural shock which I had created that day had finally ended. A violent wind- and rainstorm hit the rain forest later that night, and we slept sound like a log.

Nana Yaa Akyaa, the Queen of Ampabame (c) presenting Eva Hill, "Queen of Progress/ Development."

During my stay in Ghana, we were privileged to meet several important Ashanti leaders of the area. First to visit us was Nana Akuamoa Boateng, III, the Paramount Chief of Manso Asaman. The purpose of his visit was to inform us that he had recommended that my wife Eva be elevated to the status of "Queen of Progress/ Development" in recognition of her vision to build an Educational and Cultural Institute for Human Development on the three acres of

Nana Akuamoa Boateng, III, Paramount Chief of Manso Asaman welcoming me to Ghana.

land designated to her by the Addai family while in Ghana in August 2000. The formal ceremony for conveying this honor was held at the neighborhood school on September 16, 2001. Everyone in the town attended to watch the new village mother receive the ceremonial stool of honor. The ceremony was a most solemn affair, celebrated in great dignity, style, and dance. The ritual has created a lifelong bonding between us and the people of Ghana.

Eva receiving the "Queen of Progress/Development" award.

People of all ages were so eager to learn all they could about my family and to teach us as much as they could about themselves and their culture. I was delighted to learn from Margaret Konama, my newly adopted African sister, how people of the Ashanti Tribe are given their names. My name, for example, she advised, is Kwame Asare, because I was born on a Saturday evening during the month of September.

The enslavement of my ancestors had been a lifelong nightmare for me. Movies and television documentaries, such as *Roots, Middle Passage*, and episodes focusing on the Negro's struggle for civil rights here in America had served to reignite within me a silent rage that had compelled me to seek more knowledge about both Black history and my family of eight generations. This visit to Ghana served to temper my rage.

The final and most chilling experience that I encountered while in Ghana was my tour of the Elmina Castle, built by the Portuguese in 1482, and the surrounding Fishing Port on the River Benya estuary. Originally built as a military fortress from which to defend the Portuguese soldiers and explorers from possible outside attackers and to protect their gold and other precious metals from being seized, this dismal facility ultimately became the primary collecting and holding compound to support the rapidly growing slave trade conducted by the

Elmina Castle, built by the Portuguese in 1482, is the place where our people were held to be deported to the U.S. and sold into slavery.

Portuguese at that time. Following this brief historical background of the castle, the tour guide proceeded to lead us through the castle while carefully explaining the program operation, the specific use, and the significance of each room and the connecting areas within the Elmina Castle compound. The tour guide was a professional history teacher. His one-hour tour and the description of the castle operation traumatized my soul once again.

Appropriately selected for his position, this tour guide, a native of Ghana, exhibited deep passion and emotion while describing the cruel, deceitful, and inhumane manner in which many African people were lured or brought to the castle; the manner in which they were processed while being held; and their exit of no return from the castle

Our Elmina Castle tour guide, Mr. Korsah, explains the castle's history and operations.

175

and their own free country and homeland without having any knowledge of what was actually happening to them. With each bit of information and explanation the guide gave us, I carefully photographed the area and the location within the facility where all these horrible events and activities actually took place. The accounts of each event he gave, associated with the appearance and the atmosphere of the area within the castle, left me speechless, mentally disturbed, chilled, and emotionally dismantled. Comforted by my wife Eva, I managed to gain my composure by the end of the tour to congratulate the tour guide for a job well done. While staring each other directly in the eyes, we shook hands firmly, as if to say, "Although we both have been spared of the horrible inhumanity experienced by our early ancestors, we, as descendants of these ancestors, have both managed to survive in our respective countries, in our own time, in our own way, and in our own hearts. But it was so good for us to be reunited once again here in our native homeland."

Ironically, the historic return to my native homeland of Ghana, West Africa, had occurred during a period when my native homeland of America had been attacked by terrorists on September 11, 2001. Being separated from home and family under such horrible circumstances fills one with great anxiety. We were quite fearful that our return to America would be canceled or delayed indefinitely. This situation with which we were faced for the first time in my life enabled me to actually identify and to experience the emotional anxiety and trauma that my first-generation slave great-great-grandmother, Miriah Reese, and other captives must have experienced when they were separated from their families and deported from their native West Africa to other unknown destinations throughout the world. Their hope that someday they might find their way back home to be united with those family members they left behind was their dream that has never died.

Nana Akuamoa Boateng, III, Mamengenhene

I will always have fond memories of Ghana and the many proud and beautiful people with whom we had the pleasure of living and associating. Everything we experienced, everyone we met, and everything we saw made me proud to be of African descent. Yes, I am a member of the great Ashanti Nation of Ghana. My African name is Kwame Asare. I am also very proud to be an American whose family was given the name Hill by an unknown slaveholder who valued the quality of my earliest ancestors enough to purchase them at the slave auction that day they arrived. Subsequent years after their arrival, our family members somehow gravitated to Austin, Texas, where I was born into the fifth generation of the Reese-Chambers family in my native homeland of America.

The following photographs show additional highlights of my historical journey to West Africa, which, I hope, will inspire you to visit Africa someday yourself.

Sammy Agyekum and Irene Agyekum

Students displaying high school scholarships earned

Yams for sale at Market Square

Jim and Eva seated in King Royal Guest Chairs on the street outside the King's private home awaiting their personal meeting with Otumfuo Nana Osei Tutu, II, King of Ashanti, Ghana, West Africa.

Eva Hill is given a tour of her parcel of land by members of the Addai family to observe progress being made on her project.

Visitors from a nearby village helping to clear Eva's land for developing the Educational and Cultural Institute for Human Development project.

Gladys Appiah (center) and Linda Fosuah were awarded caps by Jim for their outstanding assistance during the visit.

Jim Hill barbecuing in Ghana on the pit he made for the occasion.

Beautiful hostesses of the Golden Beach Hotel Resort near Elmina

Second collection at Mass where people danced up the aisle to drop their money in the collection box.

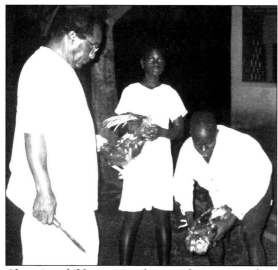

Ghanaian children assisted Jim with preparing the chickens for dinner...the most unpleasant task of all.

An elementary school in the village. Children are cleaning the campus on their first day of school.

The secret door to the Governor's bedroom in the Elmina Castle where slave women were brought up to entertain the Governor.

The torture chamber in the Elmina Castle where unruly slaves were sent to be punished, usually starved or smothered to death.

The boats utilized to transport the slaves from the castle shore to the Portuguese ships anchored offshore in the ocean.

Principles and Values

(Church, Work, and Play)

The ninth anniversary, July 29, 1996, and the thirtieth anniversary, June 24, 1996, of the deaths of Big Momma and Big Poppa were respectively observed. As I celebrated my sixtieth birthday this year, my heart beamed with great pride and honor each time I took quiet moments out of my busy day in government to reflect briefly upon my grandparents' many outstanding attributes and achievements. They lived their lives to the fullest. They raised their family of twelve through hard labor, love, and by setting good examples. They paid their poll taxes and other bills on time and voted in every public election. They dressed in loud, bright colors on Juneteenth and celebrated the Fourth of July along with all their fellow Texans. They were proud to be Black and proud to be Americans.

The church was the center of their lives. Their home, school, and the communities which they helped build became the basis of their future aspirations. I think my two grandparents were the greatest grandparents who ever lived. We all miss them so very much and wish they could be here just to see how we all are doing today.

Garfield and Marie Chambers were always so proud of their family. Their pride could easily be detected in the conversations they had with others, especially with new people whom they were meeting for the first time. Marie would always interrupt her conversations with her adult friends to introduce her children or grandchildren whenever they happened to come around. She would always include in her introductions some important things her family members had accomplished, where they were going, what they were doing, or where they lived. Garfield, a man of few words, would often show his admiration for his children and grandchildren by always greeting them with a big smile and a very brief conversation before going off to work or before resuming reading his Bible or daily newspaper. We had a way of knowing that these grandparents enjoyed having us come around by the special attention they always gave us.

I visited Blacks Memorial Baptist Church in July of 1996, along with Mother. Just knowing that this was the home church of Garfield and Marie, which they had helped build many years ago, made us both feel special and honored to be worshiping here. Only a few friends were present who knew the Chambers from years ago, but they all knew my mother and me. Flashbacks of the old community of St. John, the church, friends, and deceased loved ones who had known the greatness and the hospitality of my grandparents flooded my mind as my aging mother and I departed from the church.

Sociologically speaking, the Chambers family unit, as an institution, was deeply rooted in religious principles. The church always remained the focus of their daily lives. By no means, however, should anyone be led to believe that our grandparents were religious fanatics. While always keeping a strong faith in God, the Garfield Chambers couple also believed in hard work and the philosophy that "God helps those who help themselves." I have always tried to pattern my own life accordingly.

Jim Hill lecturing at St. George Church.

179

Jim Sr. and Jim II carrying two deer which Jim II shot with one bullet in South Carolina.

Each Sunday, while lecturing at St. George Church, in Fort Lauderdale, I am reminded of the leadership role Grandfather Garfield played while serving as deacon at Blacks Memorial Baptist Church. The annual hunting trips I take each year to South Carolina with my sons to hunt deer, wild turkeys, squirrels, and rabbits are reminiscent of the recreational activities Grandfather did with his sons when I was a young boy. I quickly discovered, as he did, that working and playing with my sons in such activities developed the foundation for a very close relationship with them, which has grown and lasted through the years. Golf outings with my daughter Eva and granddaughter Kayla bond me with the girls, as well as with my wife Eva, a retired teacher, who often joins us in these activities nowadays.

Fishing has been a favorite sport for my sons and me since they were diaper-trained. We enjoy fishing in the creeks of Texas, as well as in rivers, canals, lakes, and the Atlantic Ocean. Marie and Garfield both took me fishing at six years of age, along the Wilbarger Creek, where they lived on the Yancy Farm. Mother, along with my grandparents and neighbors, would muddy the creeks during the hot month of August when the water level in the creek was low. When they made the water hole muddy, the fish would swim to the top of the water. The group would harvest enough fish to supply the families for three months.

Jim displaying 60 lb catfish grabbed in South Carolina.

Ann and Jim showing off 7 lb bass caught two days apart.

In the late spring or summer months while in college, my son Jim and his friends would go "grabbing" in the creeks of South Carolina. This technique was not quite like "muddying," but these young men had to wade into the creek to locate large holes under tree roots near the bottom of the creek where huge catfish would be nesting. When a hole was located, one of the guys would stick his leg or arm in it in search of the fish. If a fish was felt in the hole, one of the fishermen would crawl into the hole underwater and pull it out. Pulling a sixty-pound catfish from a hole several feet underwater often resulted in a five-minute wrestle and a number of cuts and bites on the hands and bodies of the sportsmen. My grandparents were never brave enough to try such a sport, and neither am I.

Marie Chambers had a talent for growing plants and beautiful flowers. As a little boy, I learned to appreciate and admire the beautiful flower gardens she developed around her home. I learned how to grow and to care for plants from watching her. I particularly enjoyed harvesting the fruit from her trees and plucking bouquets of flowers for the house and our church. As a tribute to my grandmother today, I look forward to November and July when I can harvest oranges and mangoes from my own trees in Florida to ship to other families at home in Texas.

Oranges Jim grows at home in Fort Lauderdale are delicious.

Garfield and Marie Chambers knew the value of spending quality time with their children and grandchildren, no matter how demanding work in the fields and around the farmhouse became. Whenever we take our granddaughter Kayla and our own children to the beach, park, church, or the local zoo, we are able to experience the love and concern our grandparents always had for all of us. Every moment they took to explain

Front yard of the Hill residence in Fort Lauderdale, landscaped by Jim himself in 1992.

the nature of animals, fish, plants, birds, and people to me when I was a little boy was among the greatest learning experiences of my life, which I have never forgotten. Having their children and grandchildren spend time together visiting, playing, picnicking, or simply talking and laughing together made Marie and Garfield very happy. They would be so pleased to know how much our cousins enjoy being together as often as they can.

Kayla riding her first bicycle bought by her aunt.

Whenever Ray Westbrook, Marshall Toliver, and I get together, opportunities are often created to bring large groups of the family together to have fun. Garfield and Marie were always aware of the close bonding relationship which existed among their three grandsons. They both would be proud to know of the close relationship which still exists among us, and now with our children as well. Not a weekend passes by that Clifford does

Cousins Ray, Marshall, and Jim: "The Three Amigos."

not spend some time with his nephews and nieces. Bernice Toliver's relationship with her nieces and nephews today is as close as that of sisters and brothers. This was the type of relationship Garfield and Marie wanted for the whole family. The big brother relationship I enjoy so much with my own children today is much like the relationship Garfield had with his sons and daughters.

Clifford visits with nephews, Marshall and Ronnie Toliver.

Jim Hill with sons Dudley and Jim II working at the Boys and Girls Clubs in Davie, Florida.

Jim Hill II was inducted into the United States Army Reserve as a Second Lieutenant in June 1996. He was subsequently accepted to participate in the Army's medical school program through Nova Southeastern University. He graduated from Nova Medical School in May 2000 and was commissioned Captain in the Army Reserve the same day. He looks forward to completing residency training in May 2004 to launch his professional career as an Emergency Medical Doctor. Marie and Garfield Chambers would have been so thrilled to witness these ceremonies.

If a Black family could grow up in Bastrop County during the early 1900s, raise, educate, and prepare their twelve children for operating successfully in American society as we know it today, this family is a success. Their yesterday's style of living has shaped my style of life today. It also motivated their grandson Marshall Toliver to finally get married. What a beautiful impact on the entire Chambers family.

Marshall's wedding and family party

Having fun is one of the family's oldest traditions. I keep this tradition alive in Florida. Marshall keeps it alive in Austin, while Bernice Toliver and Clifford Chambers bring all families together for the grand old downhome parties that only they can give. 🔀

Dudley Hill, at the University of South Florida, was selected to the 1998 NCAA Division II College All American Team.

Dudley Hill poses with teammates Cliff Dell (#4) and Mike Sandy (#13) at the 1998 College All American game in Miami, Florida.

Outdoor Parties with the Kids

Going-away party with the Roberts
Family in Houston, 1975.

Annual Easter party, 13th year

Jim congratulates 1999 Champion
Easter Egg Hunters.

13th Anual Easter party hosted by the Hills

Birthday party for Kayla

Cousin Butch's New Year's Eve Party, 1991, Austin

Jean kicks things off while Vera, Bernice, and Rutherford
tune in.

Helen, Jim, and Albert sipping tea

Jim and Eva toasting New Year's 2003

Cliff, Joycelyn, and Ray get down

Ray and Jowell, New Year's 2003

Family Party with Friends Hosted by Jim and Eva, July 1996

Ann welcomes her friend from Chicago.

Eating and chatting together are old and new friends

Breanna of Austin swings new friend.

Jokes and stories spell fun

Al Brown (r) keeps party lively

Bob Wojack and coworker admiring fruit platter.

Jim and Eva, your host and hostess

Angela Bynes congratulates Broward's first lady sheriff.

Iris Greenleaf with neighbors and friends.

30

The Diversification Celebration

(A Family Renaissance: My New Beginning)

During the new millennium period (2000 to 2003), the accomplishments of a number of our family members were most remarkable. Their influence on the rest of us provoked an urge within to alter our usual way of life. On a personal note, my son Jim had graduated from medical school, and my daughter Eva and I had earned master's degrees in our respective career fields. Dudley had started his career with the Boys and Girls Clubs of Tampa, Florida, but has affiliated with the Boys and Girls Clubs of Broward County, while my wife Eva was enjoying her second year of retirement. My granddaughter, Kayla Williams, had won Golfer of the Year titles for both years from the Junior Golf Association of South Florida for girls nine to ten years of age. Bianca Taylor, our second grandchild, was born on May 8, 2001. Two years later, Faith Hill, a third granddaughter, was born on March 25, 2003.

In spite of such positive trends, however, the year 2000 had ended on a very sad note for me. Mother had spent the last two months of the year back and forth between the hospital and the nursing home. Fortunately, I had managed to spend the Christmas and New Year holidays in Austin with her. Her health had deteriorated to a point near death. Doctors had given up all hope for her recovery. I therefore had to return to Fort Lauderdale fearful that we might lose her at any time.

Upon my return to Fort Lauderdale, Dr. Chester McCulloch, a long-time Jamaican friend of mine, conveyed to me the good news that I had been selected to receive an Honorary Doctor of Humanities from Trinity International University. The official Honorary Doctorate Confirmation Service was scheduled for April 1, and I looked forward to attending.

To my great dismay and anguish, Mother passed away on March 30, 2001, just two days before the Confirmation Service. I was suddenly burdened with this dreadful dilemma: Should I remain in Fort Lauderdale and participate in the Confirmation Service, or should I return immediately to Texas to arrange for the funeral?

Fort Lauderdale Mayor Jim Naugle sponsored James Hill for the Honorary Doctor of Humanities. City Manager Floyd Johnson issued the charge.

As the family administrator and the sole surviving child, I had full responsibility for Mother's welfare and her estate. The Chambers family members were in great need of my presence at this time. However, considering the fact that I had never been a recipient of such a great honor, my decision to participate in the Confirmation Service was supported by all. Although we were greatly saddened by Mother's passing, the family was extremely proud that I was being hailed with an honorary doctorate.

I attended the Confirmation Service on April 1, knowing Mother would have wanted me to experience that special day. My family and I then left for Texas. Arrangements had been made so that we could be there for the memorial service.

Dr. James O. Hill receives hug from his son, Dr. James O. Hill II, after hooding his dad.

We spent ten days in Texas for the ceremonies and to take care of a number of important family matters. The many acts of kindness and thoughtful expressions received from the neighboring friends and relatives during the time of bereavement were strong testaments of the love and high esteem to which Ethel was held by everyone. Persons both young and old chronicled their feelings at the wake and memorial services held in memory of her. Thankful for the many years that members of the immediate Chambers family had enjoyed in this life together, the four surviving members, Henry, Mary, Clifford, and Bernice, were right there with me, and for me, providing, as always, that physical and emotional support I needed to get through the saddest days of my life.

During the relocation from her own residence to the Monte Siesta Retirement Facility on that morning of July 30, 1999, Ethel expressed to me her sincere hope that she might get well enough to return to her own home and neighborhood someday and even, perhaps, worship with her church congregation. So, in response to her wish, the memorial service commenced with an automobile procession, which proceeded from the mortuary to her residence, through the St. Johns community, and by Blacks Memorial Baptist Church, pioneered by her late father and mother, Garfield and Marie Chambers.

Our journey back to Fort Lauderdale by car was long and tiring. It gave me an opportunity to think and to reflect upon the present and my future. Often referred to by many as the "Catalyst" for change in the City of Fort Lauderdale for the past three decades, I concluded that I was finally ready to pass the baton.

Retire from the City? No! But to diversify my thirty-seven-year public service career with the general public? Yes! My continuing need and thirst for making a difference in the community and in the world would hopefully enable me to continue my efforts to make an impact on the quality of life for me and for others around me.

In recognition of my many years of service provided to the people of the Greater Fort Lauderdale/Broward County community, Discovery Cruise Lines, Fort Lauderdale Greater Sister Cities International, Charmettes of Broward County, St. George Parish, and Boys and Girls Clubs of Broward County, cosponsored with the City of Fort Lauderdale, a four-day retirement/diversification celebration from July 17 through July 20, 2001. It was the first honor of its kind in the history of the City to be given to an employee.

City Manager Floyd Johnson was Master of Ceremony for the Fort Lauderdale community reception honoring Jim.

The four-day celebration attracted over two thousand participants and included a Fort Lauderdale Beach Party on July 17, the International Friendship Cruise aboard the Discovery Cruise Lines to the Bahamas on July 18, the City of Fort Lauderdale Community Reception on July 19, and the Texas-Style Cookout at the Hill residence on July 20.

Dr. James O. Hill II introduces father, Dr. James O. Hill, Sr., at City's reception honoring Jim.

Fifty relatives and close friends from Austin and around the state of Texas attended these events in lieu of their annual family reunions. This was the first visit to Fort Lauderdale for most of them. I was so proud to be their host this year.

The only fantasy I have ever had in my lifetime was for all of my family and friends to come to Fort Lauderdale to spend at least one whole day together with me, enjoying the beautiful city I helped to build and redevelop and to meet the many wonderful people who have

Dr. Hill accompanied by his immediate family at City Reception

become such a vital part of my life the thirty-five years I have lived here. These fifty relatives and friends made my fantasy a reality – an even greater reality than I could have ever envisioned. The Garfield and Marie Chambers legacy was being manifested in everything we did those four incredible days we spent together. These two awesome grandparents of mine had taught me as a youth to value family and friends above all else, but it has taken an experience such as that provided by the people of Fort Lauderdale on the occasion of my retirement to fully comprehend the essence of their teaching. Thank you all for spending four exciting days with me here in the "Venice of America." It is the memories of those four glorious days that encouraged me to *diversify* rather than to *retire*.

There will always be love in my thoughts for each of you who helped to make my fantasy come true. Perhaps we can get together again for another visit some day, some time, and some place, real soon. It is the Chambers family way of getting to know each other, getting connected, and staying in touch.

The following photographs summarize for the reader the significant events of the four-day celebration which have served to revitalize and to stimulate hope for our future. ⬙

Jim's relatives and friends from Texas who came to Fort Lauderdale for this mini-family reunion to celebrate his retirement

Jim's International Friendship Cruise to the Bahamas and Texas-Style Cookout

Pearl Moore as "Tina Turner"

Ralph Johnson and Eva Hill.

Robert Taylor

Cousins Marshall Toliver and Henry Chambers

Connie Hoffman, former City Manager of Fort Lauderdale (center) with guests.

Ann Hill, Jim, and Charles Chambers

Bianca Taylor with grandmother, Jo Ann Taylor.

Ann and Reginold Smith, friends from Austin, Texas.

Jackie Wilson, Sandy Coleman, and Nancy Ford

Fort Lauderdale Community Reception

Dr. Hill embraces mother, Eva Mosby

Dr. Hill with members of the Harold Pearson family

Bernice, Rose Mary, Myra, and relatives

The Taylor sisters (center) flanked by Shela Williams and daughter

Ann, Shela, Leonard, and Vera

Dr. Hill's relatives and friends from Austin, Texas

Dr. Romando James and Eva Mosby.

Dr. Hill with Aunts Mary Westbrook and Bernice Toliver.

Ralph Taylor with Aunt Bernice Toliver.

The Texas Hoedown

(l to r) Joan, Warren, David and Linda Chambers, and Joycelyn Toliver

(l to r) Kathleen, Elizabeth, Erma George, and Mary Roberts

Betty Clark, Carl Mayhue, Andy, and Mrs. Collins

Dr. Cameron, guest, and Archie

Rosa Taylor and guest; Commissioner Carlton Moore

Bennie, Jim, Laura, Eva, and Deborah

Albert and Helen Patterson

Cindy Machal and guest

Paige and Erica Fleeks

The Texas Hoedown

Mr. and Mrs. Levi Henry

Dr. and Mrs. James Hill II

Dr. Bennie Moultry

Mother and daughter, Hattie and Miriam

Dr. Goldberg and Attorney Larry Gore

Marshall Toliver

Marylan and Rocky Davis

Cousins Bill Bacon and
Bernadette Caye.

(l to r) Charmettes Sandy, Nancy, and Geneva

31

The Family Hotline

(A Directory)

Calling or writing friends and loved ones is the best way we have of letting them know that we really do think about them. Visiting and spending some quality time with those we love are even better ways of reassuring them that we care. For the elderly, receiving a phone call, a simple card, or a brief visit by a young grandson, a daughter, or a friend can be as soothing and comforting as a warm ray of sunshine on a cold winter's day. Big Momma and Big Poppa were the sunshine of our lives.

Through their participation in the development of this book, each family member has made a commitment to stay in touch with each other. By sharing some of their most personal family portraits, phone numbers, addresses, and other important facts about themselves, some members who had previously felt like strangers, no longer feel that way. Greater efforts and sacrifices are now being made by each of us to attend the Chambers family reunion currently held in Austin until alternate locations are considered in the future. I cannot begin to describe how thrilling it was to call my cousins Kaye, Joy, and Kenneth Chambers, of Austin, late one night to get new phone numbers and addresses for their families. Learning about James Rivers, his son Joseph and daughter Taylor, through my cousin Gerri Nash, of Cedar Creek, really made my day on March 2, 1998, as we talked by phone. I found it very difficult to believe that I had a second cousin forty-five years of age living in California whom I never knew existed. This single experience alone demonstrated clearly to me more than anything else our family's great need for this book. Every family should have a "Hotline"!

Although the portraits, phone numbers, addresses, and other important facts about our lives will change with the passing of time, our love for each other will only grow as we continue to stay in touch. This family directory should help us to visit each other more often by conversation until that surprise visit is made in person.

This Chambers Family Directory contains the names, addresses, and phone numbers of the twelve Chambers children and those of their immediate family members. Utilizing this data, it will be possible to contact or to locate members belonging to the sixth, seventh, and eighth generations who are often more mobile at this stage of their development. I felt, however, that it was very important to list the current ages of the above three generation members so that family members or friends may have a reference point by age at the time of publication.

Grandchildren of Garfield and Marie Chambers

| *LaZelle Westbrook* | *Helen Patterson* | *Anya Taylor* | *Ericka Toliver* | *Kayla Williams* |

Granddaughters   **Great-granddaughter**   **Great-great-granddaughters**

THE CHAMBERS FAMILY DIRECTORY
1987–2004
We must always stay in touch...

PARENT	1ST COUSIN	2ND COUSIN	Age	3RD COUSIN	Age	4TH COUSIN	Age
1. *Alberta & *Allie Nash	Alfred & Garnis Octavia 600 Arbor Circle Austin, TX 78745 (512) 442-7064	Gerald Carla	37 36	Sterling Jeffery	3 16		
	*Herbert & Faye Nash 2109 Chase Circle Bryant, TX 77803 (512) 928-4416	Belinda Natlyn	36 31	Philip	3		
	Doris Nash (Claude White) 12813 Kylewich Houston, TX 77221 (713) 723-3238	Donna Claude Jr.	33 32	Jonovan Joseph Hannah Madison	11 3 6 2		
	Erma Jean George 7309 Meadowood Dr. Austin, TX 78723 (512) 926-7839	Cindy Machal	33				
	Melvin & Gerri Nash Box 800 Cedar Creek, TX 78612 (512) 303-4543	James Rivers *Herbert Kathleen Christopher	50 46 42 35	Joseph Taylor Charles McKiney Andre Jackson Cole Allen	8 6 24 19 7		
	Leonard & Elizabeth Nash 4801 Hillspring Circle Austin, TX 78721 (512) 926-3076	Tony La Shawn	34 28	Tony Tarrell Tevin White	18 13		
2. *Leon & *Ida Chambers							
3. *Henry & *Ida Chambers 2001 E. 11th St. Austin, TX 78702 (512) 472-0252							
4. *James A. & *Benjamin Roberts 3358 Airport Blvd. Houston, TX 77051 (713) 738-6708	*Benzella Roberts (McIntosh) *Venetta and David Mackey 12830 Redfern Houston, TX 77048 (713) 919-6828	Lyndia *Venetta Paul Mary Benzella Tessell *Mavis *Madeline	45 43 42 41 39 38 39 36	Lanora McDavid Garric Jennifer David Alycia *Byron Miracle Maranda Tarneta Travis	28 17 18 17 15 21 27 22 21 21 17	Shamarchs Pierra Empress	12 7 1

PARENT	1ST COUSIN	2ND COUSIN	Age	3RD COUSIN	Age	4TH COUSIN	Age
	* Bertrand H. & Doris Roberts 842 Drakestone Houston, TX 77053 (713) 433-5523	Rita	40	James	14		
		Sean A.	39	Alice	19	Corey	5 mo
				Damita	16		
		Damita	35	Justin			
				Nakiesha	22	Patrik	5
				Anitra	20	Tyler	3
				J.R.	19		
				Steven	18		
				Heather	16	Tavian	1
		Dionne	31	Michael Nolan	12		
				Aaron	11		
				Courtney	10		
	Myra L. Roberts/Fleeks P.O. Box 14015/5106 Cosby Houston, TX 77221 (713) 748-1838	Roderick	33				
		Erica	32	Paige	11		
				Cameron	6		
	John M. Roberts & *Rebecca 6824 Sherwood Houston, TX 77021 (713) 741-5522	John Jr.	37	Rochelle	15		
				Courtney	13		
				John Micah III	12		
		Bethel	33	Shanay	12		
				Candice	11		
				Patrick	10		
		Suzette	33				
5. * Ethel & *Eugene Hill *(William Hill) 7211 Providence St. Austin, TX 78752	* Minnie Hill & Oliver Taylor 5804 Boulder Creek Austin, TX 78724	Diane	47	Corbie	28	Jasmin	9
						Chester	7
				Tenya	26		
		Lester	44	Anya	20		
				Tamara	9		
				Brant	6		
		Ralph	43	Raineisha	22		
				Breanna	13		
				Dyandra	8		
		Oliver Jr.	38	Denerick	20		
	James Hill & Eva Mosby 450 N.W. 34th Avenue Ft. Lauderdale, FL 33311 (954) 583-1136	Eva Jr.	36	Kayla Williams	12		
				Bianca	2		
		James II	32	Faith	6 mo		
		Dudley	27				
6. Mary & *Ross Westbrook 417 Scott Street San Francisco, CA 94117 (415) 863-5866	LaZelle Westbrook 5038 Severance Dr. San Jose, CA 95136						
	Raymond & Velma Westbrook 417 Scott Street San Francisco, CA 94117 (415) 552-6868	Terri	36				
7. * Norris & *Elnora Chambers 6909 Providence Ave. Austin, TX 78752	Willie Norris Chambers Jr. 6909 Providence Ave. Austin, TX 78752 (512) 459-8891	Corey	27				
	Delores Chambers/Odis Jones 8201 Furness Cove Austin, TX 78753 (512) 302-3235	Odis Jr.	30	Xavier	10		
				Keiondra	3		
		Lana	26	Alicia	7		

PARENT	1ST COUSIN	2ND COUSIN	Age	3RD COUSIN	Age	4TH COUSIN	Age
	Howard Chambers/Carolyn 6909 Providence Ave. Austin, TX 78752	Keith Dexter	25 16				
	Paul Chambers/Dorothy 6915 Bethune Austin, TX 78752 (512) 302-3235	Anthony Monica Paul Jr. Mary	31 26 25 23				
8. * Thelma & Milton Allen 6905 Burnell Drive Austin, TX 78723 (512) 926-6227	Jean Allen & Rutherford Yates 6905 Burnell Drive Austin, TX 78723 (512) 926-6227						
9. * Seallen & Eunice Chambers 1706 Perez Austin, TX 78723 (512) 926-3799	* Charles C. Chambers 5205 Overbrook Austin, TX 78721 (512) 926-7448						
Lillian Chambers 4900 Carson Hill Dr. Austin, TX 78723 (512) 926-0515	Henry A. Chambers/Beverly 1600 Perez Austin, TX 78721 (512) 926-1866	Kimberly Sean	33 29	Julian Brandon	12 9		
	* David Chambers 4900 Carson Hill Dr. Austin, TX 78723 (512) 926-0515						
	* Don Chambers/Linda 179 Wahane Lane Bastrop, TX 78722	Kimberly Kinney Almuria Kinney Don Jr. Bridgette	35 34 33 29				
	Kaye Chambers Bennett 1107 Glen Summer Cove Austin, TX 78753 (512) 832-1903	Noell Crystal	25 23				
	Joy Chambers 6721 Roseborough Dr. Austin, TX 78747 (512) 292-8704	Lawrence Jeanene	25 20				
	Kenneth & Vann Chambers 4900 Carson Hill Dr. Austin, TX 78723	Kenneth Jr. James Kennisha	25 23 20				
	Roger & Vashti Chambers 4900 Carson Hill Drive Austin, TX 78723 (512) 926-0515	Erica Cataron Roger Jr.	25 23 19				
10. Clifford & *Rose Chambers 3003 E. 13th St. Austin, TX 78702 (512) 476-8929	Dwight Chambers 3003 E. 13th St. Austin, TX 78702 (512) 476-8929						
	Nell Chambers 3003 E. 13th St. Austin, TX 78702 (512) 476-8929						

PARENT	1ST COUSIN	2ND COUSIN	Age	3RD COUSIN	Age	4TH COUSIN	Age
11. * Floyd & Allene Chambers 3403 Norwood Hill Austin, TX 78723 (512) 926-9566 (512) 928-0756	Helen Chambers/ Albert Patterson 7210 Marywood Circle Austin, TX 78723	Traci Kedric	34 31				
	Charles C. Chambers/Joan 7008 Shumard Circle Austin, TX 78759-4647 (512) 258-2415	Warren	19				
	Shirley Chambers/ Gerald Daniels 4122 Robin Drive Grand Perrie, TX 75052 (972) 237-9499	Kevin Gerald Jr. Samuel	30 28 23	Noah Jasmine Paige	1 2 1		
	Samuel Chambers/Tina 8409 Saber Creek Trail Austin, TX 78759 (512) 335-7228						
	Michael Chambers/Janie 8405 Valley Field Austin, TX 78723	Sade	17				
12. Bernice & *Olen Toliver 6809 Willamette Drive Austin, TX 78723 (512) 926-5282	Marshall & Joycelyn Toliver 3724 Geese Roundrock, TX (512) 716-1068	Ericka Trey	33 29	Skye	10		
	Ronald & Cheryl Toliver 1904 Winsong Dallas, TX 75081 (214) 235-4725	Erica	25	Corey LaKayla	3 1		

* Denotes deceased.

32

Landmarks of Time

(A Living Memorial)

The old cliché, "out of sight, out of mind," has little or no relevance to the Chambers family. Our thirty-six deceased relatives are still very much with us in thought and in spirit. They always will be. Their legacies shall continue to provide inspiration for both the young and the old among us. The contributions they made to their immediate families, friends, and the community will long be remembered and looked back upon with favor, pride, and honor.

By the time I had finished writing this book, twenty-one of our family jewels were missing from our treasure. Grandmother Marie (Big Momma) had lived to be 103. Great-grandmother Lilia outlived her daughter by seven years. She died at age 110. Longevity has been a dominant trademark of the Chambers family for over a century. Perhaps the secret of longevity is to be found somewhere in our understanding of the type and the quality of lifestyles they lived.

The years passed by so quickly. We have scattered ourselves throughout the United States. Funeral services of our family members were held at times and places we could not always attend, but we all wanted to be there to console. The roll call and the photographs we have taken of the family memorials shall serve as important symbols and landmarks for our family members, friends, and all others to know and to remember who we are, when we lived, and when we died. Hopefully, the contributions we have made to our families and to society during our lifetime will be recorded in the hearts and the minds of those who benefited and will be acceptable in the eyes of the Good Lord.

We, the living members of the Chambers family, do hereby rededicate ourselves to the proposition that no members of this family will ever be forgotten. ▨

Clifford Chambers, retired

We will always treasure, love, and cherish so much...

Bernice Toliver, retired educator, Austin Independent Schools.

Cameron Fleeks, seventh-generation representative.

Jim Hill

"Our Landmark"

CHAMBERS
IN LOVING MEMORY

GARFIELD
MARCH 4, 1883
JUNE 24, 1966

MARIE
MAY 7, 1884
JULY 29, 1987

Family Memorial Roll Call

Great-Great-Grandparents	Miriah Chambers	Date Unknown
Great-Grandparents	Peter Reese	March 3, 1932
	Lilia Reese	August 20, 1957
Grandparents	Garfield Chambers	June 24, 1966
	Marie Chambers	July 29, 1987
Uncles	Benjamin Roberts	November 16, 1962
	Eugene J. Hill	November 23, 1976
	Leon Chambers	April 9, 1977
	Norris Chambers	April 11, 1978
	Floyd Chambers	July 6, 1978
	Olen Toliver	October 2, 1986
	Seallen Chambers	April 22, 1988
	William Hill	April 23, 1989
	Allie Nash	November 7, 1991
	Ross Westbrook	October 18, 1993
	Henry Chambers	December 31, 2001
Aunts	Thelma Allen	October 13, 1980
	Ida Chambers	October 6, 1981
	Rose Chambers	June 27, 1983
	James A. Roberts	November 9, 1989
	Alberta Nash	March 19, 1997
	Ethel Hill	March 30, 2001
	Elnora Chambers	December 25, 2002
Cousins	Herbert J. Nash	May 28, 1976
	Mavis McIntosh	March 7, 1980
	Benzella McIntosh	September 14, 1980
	Tommie Hill	January 17, 1985
	Minnie Hill Crothers	December 24, 1993
	Rebecca Roberts	October 17, 1995
	Mae Nash	June 5, 1996
	Madeline Roberts	December 23, 1997
	Byron Roberts	April 5, 1998
	Venetta Mackey	June 9, 2000
	David Chambers	November 18, 2000
	Don Chambers	May 8, 2003
	Charles C. Chambers	July 6, 2003
	Bertrand Roberts	April 10, 2004
	Herbert Nash	September 25, 2004

Our parents, Eugene and Ethel Hill and James and Eva Mosby, our grandparents, Garfield and Marie Chambers, as well as aunts and uncles and the Austin-St. Johns community, have contributed to the enrichment of our lives in so many different ways. It is a debt that can never be forgotten nor fully repaid. However, there is just one small way we wanted to express our appreciation.

Therefore, in recognition of the support and contributions to all the members of our families and others, plans have been completed for developing the HILL MOSBY CHAMBERS (H.M.C.) Landmark Villa project, a four-unit single-family housing community with beautiful landscaped gardens and walkways, in their honor as our reasonable assurance that the love and many sacrifices they made for all of their children, grandchildren, and others will continue to make a difference in people's lives today and in the future.

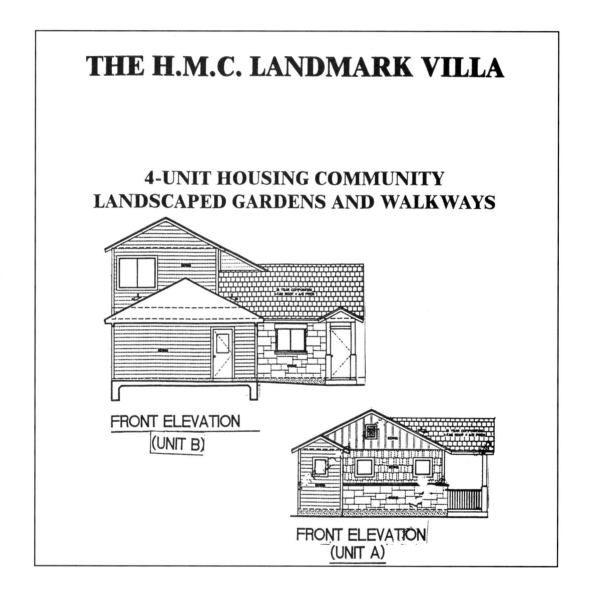

THE H.M.C. LANDMARK VILLA

4-UNIT HOUSING COMMUNITY
LANDSCAPED GARDENS AND WALKWAYS

FRONT ELEVATION
(UNIT B)

FRONT ELEVATION
(UNIT A)

HOMES: Project expected to reflect neighborhood's growing diversity

Continued from B1

homes in the neighborhood, which is mostly east of Interstate 35, south of U.S. 183 and west of Cameron Road. Hill hopes the homes, which he wants to rent to low-income families, serve as a model community within a community.

The half-million-dollar project is dedicated to Hill's parents, who were among the first African Americans to own a home in St. John. They built it in 1942 with their savings from years of picking cotton as sharecroppers. The project also honors Hill's grandparents, the Chamberses, and the parents of his wife, Eva, the Mosbys, who were also fixtures in the St. John neighborhood.

"You achieve what you did on the backs of somebody else," Hill said during a Monday morning ceremony at a St. John church. "Unless you won the lottery, somebody else is responsible for your success."

Hill said he hopes the project will serve as a point of pride in a neighborhood that has undergone much change in the past 20 years. What was once a largely African American neighborhood is now 64 percent Hispanic and home to many recent Mexican immigrants.

He envisions homes that will reflect that newfound diversity. He wants to rent out the units, which will go for below market value, to a wide array of people: African Americans, Latinos, families with children and people with disabilities. Above all, he said, the tenants must share his vision of a dynamic and integrated community. "I want to get people who understand the philosophy of what we're trying to achieve," he said.

Hill, who is writing a history of the St. John neighborhood, will occupy one of the homes.

Construction is scheduled to begin this summer, and the homes will be built in two phases. The project, which Hill said is not intended to make a profit, is being financed by Frost Bank and $38,000 of Hill's money.

The homes are being built under the City of Austin's SMART Housing program, which waives fees and speeds up the development process for

Deborah Cannon AMERICAN-STATESMAN

James and Eva Hill hope the homes they are building will serve as a point of pride in the changing St. John neighborhood.

homes that meet the city's green building and accessibility criteria and are aimed at lower-income residents. Hill estimates that the program will save the project about $15,000.

Travis County Commissioner Ron Davis said the project is an

illustration of the importance of returning to one's roots. "It means so much to this community that people have not forgotten who they are or what this community is about," he said.

jschwartz@statesman.com; 445-3616

This homecoming comes with homes

Couple returns to St. John neighborhood with building plans

By Jeremy Schwartz
AMERICAN-STATESMAN STAFF

Most housing developments don't start with a church service. But the Hill, Mosby, Chambers Memorial Landmark Villa isn't your typical

project.

More than 30 years after he left town for a successful career that included 17 years as assistant city manager in Fort Lauderdale, Fla., James Hill returned to the St. John neighborhood where he was raised with plans to give something back.

On Monday, he and his family broke ground on four

See **HOMES**, B5

Tuesday, January 6, 2004

33

Family Highlights

(Significant Family Events and Triumphs)

The sorrowful occasion of Marie Chambers' passing on July 29, 1987, had served to bring our family together in large numbers for the first time ever that I can remember. It was this single event that motivated me to start writing this book. Ironically, in October 1993, just six years later, I was summoned back to Texas once again on a sorrowful occasion to be with my sister Minnie, who appeared to be losing her three-year bout with cancer. Minnie had been hospitalized for several days, was in a slight coma, could barely open her eyes, and could not speak. My arrival and visit with her created a miracle. She made a miraculous comeback during my three-day stay in Texas.

This brief visit with Minnie was interrupted by yet another tragedy in the family, the death of Uncle Ross Westbrook on October 18, 1993. I had an urgent desire to be of comfort to both my mother and the Westbrook family during this time of bereavement. I flew to San Francisco to attend Uncle Ross's funeral and returned to Austin that next day. Upon my return to Austin from San Francisco, I was thrilled beyond words to discover that Minnie was strong enough to talk with me. I concluded this visit with a family prayer at her bedside and began to prepare for my flight back to Fort Lauderdale. That was the last time I saw my sister alive. The combination of these two major events caused me to take an even broader look at our family and at what was happening to all of us.

As our family had begun to mature, the mortality rate had finally become of noticeable significance. Minnie passed away on December 24, 1993. My father-in-law, James Mosby, passed on May 26, 1994. My mother Ethel, Aunts Mary Westbrook and Alberta Nash, and mother-in-law Eva Mosby, were all faced with the problems experienced by many aging widows and now required all the love and support our families could possibly provide. Eight years had brought about a number of changes in the lives of many younger members of our family as well. Henry and Clifford Chambers, Marshall Toliver, and I had all undergone surgery of some type, but all were well and going strong once again. As I look back to that day we buried Grandmother Chambers, I now appreciate, more than ever before, the decision I had made to write this documentary account of the Chambers family. Through this instrument, our family had already begun to reap some of every benefit for which we had hoped.

First, our family members had become better acquainted not only with the names of each relative but also with each personality, special interest, locations, and type of work and talents each exhibits. All had begun to appreciate and to become better acquainted with our incredible grandparents. The family roots, who we are, from where we had come, and the directions we are traveling today are all questions that have now become more meaningful to each of us. We are now more eager to know the answers to these questions and are more willing to seek the knowledge about our family heritage wherever it may be found. This family is committed to continuing its search for knowledge about ourselves and our ancestors. The 1995 New Year's Party in Austin, Texas, hosted by Marshall and Joycelyn, brought our family members another step closer to achieving our ultimate goal of enjoyment and maybe even understanding how the wrapping of twelve black-eyed peas in a cabbage leaf and folding it in foil paper on New Year's Eve could possibly bring one good luck during

Marshall Toliver's 1995 New Year's Party for family

The Jim Hill Family 2004: Front Row (l to r) granddaughter Kayla, Dad, granddaughters Bianca and Faith, Mom; Back Row (l to r) son-in-law Moses Taylor and wife Eva, son Dudley, daughter-in-law Ann and husband James Hill II.

the New Year. Are we superstitious or something? No, not really, because the old custom of eating black-eyed peas and rice on New Year's day that Big Momma and Big Poppa had practiced for years is also being followed while we still await our luck to win the lottery or something big.

What had originally started out to be only an ordinary family directory of names, addresses, and phone numbers, has, in just sixteen short years, developed into something far greater, more comprehensive, and more challenging than we had ever anticipated. Regrettably, a few members of the family have passed away. However, new members have been born, not to take the place of our old, but instead to fulfill and to enrich our family dreams and aspirations.

Inspiration for writing this chapter of the book came to me while in-flight to San Francisco to attend Uncle Ross's funeral. As the plane glided through the western, gold, sunlit evening skies high above the Rockies, I quickly recalled that it was thirty-eight years ago that the Westbrooks had encouraged me to leave home at seventeen years of age in search of a future for myself, to come West! The Westbrooks also introduced me to Lottie and James Caldwell, whom I will never forget, and who provided support for me when I needed it so badly as a young adult growing up in a big city while earning my own way through college. All these years later I was returning to say goodbye and to thank Uncle Ross for the love and the kindness he always extended to me and to all the cousins.

The Chambers family has always been my strongest anchor of support. Mother Ethel gave me the inspiration and the emotional stability necessary for keeping me focused in this turbulent environment such as we live in today. My sister Minnie is missed so greatly by all of us, but, especially, by her grandniece, Kayla Marie Williams, who was only two years old at the time of her death. Bianca, Kayla's two-year-old sister, is now learning to identify family members by photographs, one great value of this book.

Love of God, love of the church, of friends, and of family are the priceless jewels to be found in the Chambers Family Treasure which Garfield and Marie Chambers so carefully cultivated, developed, exhibited, and valued during their lifetime. Their virtues are for us to emulate and preserve. As an adult, I have learned to value these jewels by trying to reflect each one of them in my daily life at the workplace, in the community, my home, and in all of my relationships with people I meet daily. It was through these values that I acquired and developed my professional skills, patience, tolerance of others, and perseverance which helped sustain me the thirty years I worked in government.

Now, therefore, let it be resolved, that a candle shall be lighted or a tree planted at our family reunion each year in memory of our deceased. Our newly born shall be warmly greeted, and each of our family members shall remain forever treasured in our hearts. Strengthened by the commitment our family made sixteen years ago to get to know each other better, we hope that the readers of this book will be inspired to do the same. Black families have played a significant role in the development of this country, America, its rural and urban communities alike. Learning about your own family roots can be both rewarding and inspirational. It makes Africa and our African heritage become more meaningful and alive.

We must always remember that our great-great-grandparents, like so many other immigrants who were brought to America unwillingly, as well as those who came voluntarily, were not always well-versed in the Constitution, the Bill of Rights, or any other historical document which forms the foundation of this society. However, they all understood the spirit for which these documents stand. In order to continue our transcendence, like our early ancestors, we, too, must maintain that same spirit that carried them forward from that first day of so long ago when they arrived in the United States. It is that same spirit that led our Founding Fathers to write as part of the Declaration of Independence "that all men are created equal, that they are endowed by their creator with certain unalienable rights, that among these are life, liberty and the pursuit of happiness."

Since emancipation of the eight generations of our family lineage has occurred over a period of 173 years, I urge each of you today to pause and to ask yourself how long it has taken you to kick-start your own life and career as a free American. For some family members, it took only a few years; for others, at least ten years. Maybe, for some, like me, it took close to fifty years or longer. Think how far you have come. Think of how much you have accomplished.

While we pause on this 19th day of June 2003 (Juneteenth) to celebrate the freeing of slaves in America by President Abraham Lincoln on June 1, 1963, through passage of the Emancipation Proclamation, you must be aware of the many forms of slavery that still exist in our world today. Remember, also, that in almost every culture in the world there has been some form of slavery. Never forget that when the world is changing rapidly, slavery is changing rapidly as well.

In his book entitled *New Slavery*, Kevin Bales explores in great detail the many forms of slavery. Through this book we can expand our knowledge and our awareness of slavery and what each one of us can do to help eliminate slavery wherever we find it.

As Black immigrants and African Americans, we feel we can conquer all the odds. We have conquered oppression, domination, solitude, hunger, and feelings of despair which have been associated with our lives wherever we have lived. If there is a country in the world that stands out as an example of how human beings under such circumstances can live with dignity, that country is ours, the United States of America. Today, some authorities contend that the American family is currently in a state of decline and has all but been lost. I contend, however, in contrast, that the American family, although weakened, is still both viable and capable of enduring. I am the person I am today because of family and friends, a good person, a person with principles and values, and, above all, a family man. I sincerely hope that the information I have shared with you about our family will inspire you to share the great treasures of your own families with others. If you feel that your family members have been lost, go find them. Search for them high and low, whatever it takes to find them. Once you find them, strengthen your relationship with them by providing all the love and support you are willing to generate. You will find these tasks to be easy, just as I did, but, first, you must start.

Along these lines, I must apologize to all my relatives and friends for my delay in not publishing this book until the year 2004. My vision of the future, however, compelled me to provide additional opportunity to reflect upon the new millennium, the twenty-first century, and the challenges I feel it presents for each of us. Consider, for example, the great impact modern technology has had on the way we do things. Our grandparents would have been overwhelmed by these vast and amazing accomplishments.

Computer technology has enabled people to communicate with others quicker and more efficiently than ever before. We are now able to create richly formatted word processing, spreadsheets, e-mail, calendar and presentation documents, as well as to send and to receive these documents over the Internet. Isn't this all exciting?

It is my deepest hope that with the advent of these valuable innovations, our family, and families all over the world, will enter into the twenty-first century with a renewed commitment to attend to the needs of all its members. This institution of "Family" was created as the strongest primary, social, and cultural group among all others. This attention to family should include quality time together and a life of quality that will serve to strengthen the family position. As a new author, it is my mission to encourage and to embrace all efforts to perpetuate this dynamic family institution, with my head held high as a proud family member, just like the late James Arthur Garfield and Marie Chambers did.

Incredible as all of these inventions have been, however, as emancipated freed citizens now living in America at the dawn of the twenty-first century, we must pause to ask ourselves several rather important questions about our future: What are the most important issues that should be at the forefront of Black America's agenda today? What strategies or plans could we develop to address the important issues of our time? What issues and strategies should descendants of the Reese-Chambers generations be identifying and addressing for the future?

Some possible answers to these questions were suggested in a recent survey conducted by Steven Mintz and Susan Kellogg, leading sociologists on American Black families. According to the survey, 7 out of 10 Black children are born today without the presence of a man in the house. Many Blacks do not know the power they possess to change things and often lack the courage to try to do so. We sometimes fail to realize that leadership is obtained by service to others, not by one's age. Faith in the family has deteriorated, and trust is so difficult to convey to friends and foes.

A Black Issue Forum coordinated by Tavis Smiley, Black Entertainment Television news personality, was aired on February 2 and 3, 2001. The program featured over twenty Black leader representatives from the major public and private sectors of America. They were questioned on the principal problems and issues confronting Black Americans today. Following their discussions on the topic, the members of the forum unanimously agreed that Black America's agenda for the future must include the following issues: (1) education, (2) economic growth, (3) health, (4) the family, (5) public policy, (6) representation, and (7) voting rights. This distinguished panel of modern-day Black leaders unanimously concurred that a plan of action or strategy must be developed to address each item.

I totally agree with the findings and recommendations of this panel of concerned leaders. I therefore urge each member of the Reese-Chambers generations and all families throughout America and the world to make these issues their highest priority during this decade. Please join with me in the launching of my Family Networking Initiative Program (FNIP).

Bibliography

Adero, Malaika. *Up South*. New York: New Press, 1993.

Amneus, Daniel. *The Garbage Generation*. Alhambra, Calif.: Primrose Press, 1990.

Artlip, Mary Ann, James Artlip, and Earl S. Saltzman. *The New American Family*. Lancaster, Pa.:
    Starburst Publishers, Inc., 1993.

Bales, Kevin. *New Slavery*. Santa Barbara, Calif.: ABC-CLIO, Inc., 2000.

Barker, Eugene C., ed. *The Papers of Stephen F. Austin*, vol. II. Washington, D.C.:
    The American Historical Association, 1928.

Bateman, Audray, "Black orphanage," *The Austin American-Statesman*, 17 June, 1977, sec. 1A, p. 3.

Blockson, Charles L. *The Underground Railroad*. New York: Prentice-Hall Press, 1987.

Boles, John B. *Black Southerners 1619-1869*. Lexington, Ky.: University Press of Kentucky, 1984.

Bontemps, Arma Wendell. *100 Years of Negro Freedom*. New York: The New York Public Library, 1913.

Bornet, Vaughn Davis. *The Presidency of Lyndon B. Johnson*. Lawrence, Kan.:
    University Press of Kansas, 1983.

Campbell, Ralph B. *An Empire for Slavery: The Peculiar Institution in Texas, 1821-1865*. Baton Rouge, La.:
    Louisiana State University Press, 1989.

Davidson, Basil. *The Lost Cities of Africa*. U.S.A.: Little, Brown and Company in association with
    The Atlantic Monthly Press, 1981.

DeMorse, Charles. Clarksville *Northern Standard*. 19 February 1989.

Duret, Daphne, "S. Florida descendants honor survivors of slave trade's Middle Passage in Dade,"
    The Herald, 23 June 2003, sec. B, p. 6.

Franklin, John Hope. *From Slavery to Freedom: A History of Negro Americans*. New York:
    Knopf Publishers, 1980.

Furnas, J. C. *Goodbye To Uncle Tom*. New York: W. Sloane Associates, 1956.

Gordon, Michael. *The American Family In Social Historical Perspective*, 3d ed. New York:
    St. Martin's Press, Inc., 1983.

Haley, Alex. 1976. *Roots*. U.S.A.: Doubleday Publishing, Inc. Reprint, 1977.

Houck, J. F. *The Tree*, N.p., n.d.

Johnson, Charles. *Middle Passage*. New York: Atheneum, 1990.

Johnson, Edward A. 1911. *A School History of the Negro Race in America From 1619-1890*. New York: AMS Press. Reprint, 1969.

Kwadwo, Osei. *An Outline of Asante History, Part 1*, 2d ed. Kumasi, West Africa: O. Kwadwo Enterprise Wiamoase-Ashanti, 1994.

La Haye, Tim F. *The Battle for the Family*. Old Tappan, N.J.: Fleming H. Revell Co., 1982.

Mintz, Steven, and Susan Kellogg. *Domestic Revolutions: A Social History of American Family Life*. New York: The Free Press, 1988.

Onwubiko, K.B.C. *School Certificate: History of West Africa From AD 1000-1800*, Book One. Onitsha, Nigeria: Africana-FEP Publishers Ltd., 1967.

Salk, Lee. *Familyhood: Nurturing the Values That Matter*. New York: Simon & Schuster, 1988.

Schwartz, Jeremy. "This homecoming comes with homes," *The Austin American-Statesman,* 6 January 2004, sec. B, p. 5.

Simond, Ada D. *Looking Back: A Black Focus on Austin's Heritage, 1984*. Austin, Tex.: The Austin Independent School District and The Austin American Statesman, 1987.

Skolnick, Arlene S., and Jerome H. Skolnick. *Family In Transition*, 5th ed. Berkeley: University of California, 1986.

Smiley, Tavis. "Making Black America Better," *Jet* (February 26, 2001): file://A:\Article%2022.htm [2003, June 30].

Stampp, Kenneth M. *The Causes of the Civil War Revised*. Englewood Cliffs, N.J.: Prentice-Hall. Inc., 1974.

Swan, Ruth Rice. *A History of Black Africans*. New York: Vantage Press, Inc., 1993.

The Arthur A. Schomburg Center for Research in Black Culture. *60th Anniversary Tribute*. New York: The New York Public Library, 1986.

Thompson, Daniel C. *Sociology of the Black Experience*. Westport, Conn.: Greenwood Press, 1974.

Trepagnier, Peggy. "A Visit with Isom and Viola Reese." *Sayersville Historical Association Bulletin*, no. 2 (1982): 2-3.

U.S. *Constitution. The Constitution of The United States of America*. Bedford, Mass.: Applewood Books, n.d.

Vile, John R. *The United States Constitution*: Questions and Answers. Westport, Conn.: Greenwood Press, 1998.

Weeks, William F., reporter. *Debates of the Texas Convention*. Houston: 1846.

Support

Hello James:

To have been included among the many family groups highlighted in *Emancipation of Eight Generations*, The Chambers Family Treasure, your first literary undertaking, is a most cherished encounter. This recording of our colorful family history and legacy serves to motivate those living members of the family while memorializing our departed loved ones.

The Hill Family Enterprise concept of utilizing this memoir as a tool for the launching of a national Family Network Initiative Program (FNIP) designed specifically to strengthen family relationships through increased family awareness and appreciation provides a unique opportunity for the John H. Hill Family to assist you in addressing this important universal need.

We, therefore, wish to congratulate you and thank you on behalf of our entire network for the foresight, love, and devotion displayed throughout your endeavor.

Devotedly yours,

The Members,
John H. Hill Family

YELLOW CAB COMPANY

P. O. Box 950
Ft. Lauderdale, FL 33302
(954) 565-8900
(954) 566-1867 fax

Yellow Cab Letter of Support

Dear Jim:

Congratulations on the successful launching of your new career as a writer and publisher.

Since your arrival in Fort Lauderdale in 1968, you have served government and the people of South Florida with great distinction and honor. Much evidence of your accomplishments may be observed throughout the city from the eastern shore of our beautiful beach to the western eclipse of the Florida Everglades.

Your vision of creating a family network initiative to educate and strengthen family relationships is one of the greatest challenges facing this country today. Your book, *Emancipation of Eight Generations*, is a most remarkable motivational tool for the accomplishment of your goals.

May you reap much satisfaction from this new quest.

Sincerely,

Jesse P. Gaddis

Jesse P. Gaddis
President

GREATER FORT LAUDERDALE
sister cities international

January 28, 2005

Dear Dr. Hill:

Congratulations on the successful launching of your new career as a writer and publisher.

As you are aware from over thirty years of work and association with us, Greater Fort Lauderdale Sister Cities International (GFLSCI) is a nonprofit citizen diplomacy network dedicated to creating and strengthening partnerships between Fort Lauderdale and cities around the world, in an effort to increase global friendship and cooperation on many levels.

Emancipation of Eight Generations: The Chambers Family Treasure, your first literary undertaking, is so well-timed for all families throughout our country today. The Hill Family Enterprise concept of utilizing *Emancipation of Eight Generations* for the launching of a national Family Network Initiative Program (FNIP) designed specifically to educate and strengthen family relationships has broad global implications which compliment The Greater Fort Lauderdale Sister Cities and The Thomas McCormick Scholarship Fund for the Youth Ambassador program.

You should know that The Greater Fort Lauderdale Sister Cities is extremely proud to have you as a member of its group and will support the FNIP jointly with you in every way it possibly can.

May you reap much satisfaction from this new quest.

Sincerely,

Nuccia McCormick
Chairman Emeritus

211

Gill Hotels Company
P. O. Box 21277
Fort Lauderdale, Florida 33335
Phone: (954) 525-3451 Fax: (954) 524-2935

February 8, 2005

Mr. James Hill
PO Box 1448
Fort Lauderdale, FL   33302

Dear Jim:

Our heartiest congratulations! The genesis of your new career as a writer and publisher is both a credit to you and to our community.

Emancipation of Eight Generations, The Chambers Family Treasure, your first foray into professional writing, provides an abundance of personal experiences and information about you and your family members that should serve to both motivate and strengthen other families throughout our community and the world, just as it did for you and yours.

During the past several years, Gill Hotels, in concert with other members of the local hospitality industry and government, has done much to attract family reunion groups to South Florida. This year, South Florida rose to national popularity for attracting such groups. The Hill Family Enterprise concept of utilizing *Emancipation of Eight Generations* as the educational tool for launching a national Family Network Initiative Program (FNIP) designed specifically to educate and strengthen family relationships should complement these efforts.

Gill Hotels applauds you for undertaking a new and very worthwhile vocation. By working together, we can help you to continue to perform the kind of service this community has seen you perform for so many years.

Sincerely,

Linda L Gill
President and C.E.O. of Gill Hotels

(S) Sheraton Yankee Trader Beach Hotel
312 N. FORT LAUDERDALE BEACH BOULEVARD, FORT LAUDERDALE, FL 33304
PHONE: (954) 467-1111 FAX: (954) 462-2342

(S) Sheraton Yankee Clipper Beach Hotel
1140 SEABREEZE BOULEVARD, FORT LAUDERDALE, FL 33316
PHONE: (954) 524-5551 FAX: (954) 523-5376

Dr. Henry W. Mack, Ph.D.
6590 S.W. 13th Street
Plantation, Florida, 33317-5154
(954) 791-1816, Fax (954) 791-9131
<u>***hmack4@comcast.net***</u>

Mr. James O. Hill
P.O. Box 1448
Fort Lauderdale, FL 33302

Dear Jim,

Since your Career Diversification Celebration July 17-20, 2001, honoring your retirement from public service, you have taken another big step in your life toward becoming an author and publisher. Congratulations!!!

You served the Boys' and Girls Clubs of America and the City of Fort Lauderdale with great honor and distinction. Some of those years were rough, but this was what you wanted.

During conversations between you, other colleagues, and myself, you always spoke of the challenge of empowerment. Your face would glow as you anticipated giving to people the thrill you found in learning and accomplishing new feats.

Completing you first book, Emancipation of Eight Generations, has been a long hard pull I would imagine, but you persevered. Efficiency accompanied by courtesy and humility is a rare combination in today's world. You have been blessed to have all. You will continue to have my support, as always, in your quest to be the best at everything you undertake in the future.

May God Forever Bless You.

Henry W. "Hank" Mack, Ph.D.

Dear Jim,

Historically, from the outset of the early 1770s, there have been mutual conditions that unite Native Americans and African Americans. Both have been ill-treated and have been looked down upon by government officials from the courthouse to the White House. In Florida, Louisiana and Texas, African slaves and Native Americans united and observed each other's sufferings. What emerged from these experiences, however, was a saga of enslavement, flight, exile and ultimately, freedom.

Mr. Hill, as you know, your relationship with the Seminole Tribe of Florida goes back many years. During my term as a president of the Seminole Tribe, you played a significant role in helping to organize the Seminole Historical Society of Hollywood. The Fort Lauderdale Historical Society designated you as winner of the Byron Snyder Award in 1990, presented annually to the one individual who made the most significant contribution to preservation of the city's and the county's heritage.

To commemorate that unforgettable, friendly relationship forged between our early ancestors many years ago, the Seminole Tribe of Florida is proud to acknowledge your outstanding accomplishment of completing your new book, <u>Emancipation of Eight Generations, The Chambers Family Treasure.</u> This intriguing book illustrates how Blacks now living in today's non-segregated society fifty years after the 1954 U.S. Supreme Court decision which ended segregation in America. What great strength your family has demonstrated.

May this custom made Seminole TIKI HUT that my company has built for you and your family serve as a lasting symbol of our friendship and the mutual support we have pledged to each other and the people we proudly serve. Let us continue, then, as brothers to reflect upon our proud past as we contemplate our bright and prosperous future.

Sincerely,

Joe Dan Osceola, Ambassador and Past President, Seminole Tribe of Florida

MCWHITE'S FUNERAL HOME

Dear Dr. Hill:

Emancipation of Eight Generations, The Chambers Family Treasure, is a road map that may be followed by other families desiring to become better acquainted with members of their family tree. It is a recording of a colorful family history which strives to motivate those living members of the group while memorializing the deceased loved ones.

The Hill Family Enterprise concept of incorporating Emancipation of Eight Generations with your launching of a national Family Network Initiative Program (FNIP) designed specifically to educate and strengthen family relationships provides a unique opportunity for McWhite's Funeral Home to assist you in this effort as a part of its primary mission of memorializing.

As a former club member of the North West Unit of Boys and Girls Clubs of Broward County, which you pioneered and directed in 1968, I am proud to congratulate you for the completion of your first literary undertaking and to thank yo for all you did to motivate me to become the successful businessman I am today.

I pledge my full support of your new endeavor. Best wishes for your continued success.

Sincerely,

A. R. McWhite

Albert R. McWhite, President

3501 West Broward
Boulevard
Fort Lauderdale, Florida
33312
Phone: 954-584-0047
Fax: 954-584-7741
Email:

Mc White's Funeral Home …

Because Families Deserve the Best

Significant Contributors

Initial start-up capital and other invaluable support provided by the following contributors will underwrite the cost of printing and binding 10,000 copies of this book, which have been pledged as donations to members of the Boys and Girls Clubs of America, other deserving youth and adult organizations throughout the United States, selective foreign countries, and U.S. Military Armed Forces.

Rev. Martin Adu
North Miami, FL

Dr. & Mrs. Charles W. Akins
Austin, TX

Gloria M. Aldridge, Esq.
Houston, TX

Mr. & Mrs. Hugh Anderson
Fort Lauderdale, FL

Dr. & Mrs. William Bacon
Nashville, TN

Mary A. Becht
Tamarac, FL

Barbara Bridgewater, Esq.
Berkeley, CA

Ms. Laura Martin Bryant
Lauderhill, FL

Dr. & Mrs. Eric Cameron
Plantation, FL

Mr. Clifford Chambers & Family
Austin, TX

Rev. Dr. George Clark
Austin, TX

Mr. & Mrs. Jennings Coleman
Fort Lauderdale, FL

Mr. John Cooney
Lauderdale by the Sea, FL

Mr. Robert O. Cox
Fort Lauderdale, FL

Dr. & Mrs. Exalton A. Delco, Jr.
Austin, TX

Ms. Jowell Dixon
Austin, TX

Dr. & Mrs. Bobby Drayton
Baltimore, MD

Mr. Roy G. Elder
Austin, TX

Mr. & Mrs. Hamilton Foreman
Fort Lauderdale, FL

Mr. & Mrs. Brian & Rebecca Gamble
Donaln, SC

Mr. & Mrs. Henry Graham
Hollywood, FL

Mr. & Mrs. Ross Grooms
Fort Lauderdale, FL

Mayor Mims Hackett
Orange, NJ

Ms. Carole Hall
Detroit, MI

Mr. & Mrs. Levi Henry
Whiteville, NC

Mr. & Mrs. Harold Hill
Suisun, CA

Dr. & Mrs. James L. Hill
Austin, TX

Mr. Will Hill
Austin, TX

Mr. & Mrs. Melvin Houston
Port Arthur, TX

Mr. & Mrs. William Hutchinson, Esq.
Parkland, FL

Dr. & Mrs. Romando James
Clemson, SC

Mrs. Evelyn Lewis
Fort Lauderdale, FL

Mr. & Mrs. Minnie Stocton Mann
Austin, TX

Mr. Thomas K. McCawley
Fort Lauderdale, FL

Mr. & Mrs. T.A. McDonald
Austin, TX

Ms. Rosemary McQuay
Plantation, FL

Mr. & Mrs. Willie Mercer
Austin, TX

Mrs. Rose L. Merritt
Fort Lauderdale, FL

Dr. Dorsey C. Miller
Parkland, FL

Mr. Sam Morrison
Fort Lauderdale, FL

Mrs. Eva M. Mosby & Family
Austin, TX

Mr. & Mrs. Harold Pearson & Family
Plantation, FL

Ms. Bernadette Phifer
Austin, TX

Rev. & Mrs. R.J. Reese
Austin, TX

Mr. Joseph A. Reid
Austin, TX

Ms. Lorraine M. Salahuddin
Fort Lauderdale, FL

Mr. Marvin Sanders
Fort Lauderdale, FL

Mr. & Mrs. Reginold Smith
Austin, TX

Mr. & Mrs. Carl Solomon
Wichita Falls, TX

Mr. & Mrs. Ralph Thomas
Maplewood, NJ

Mr. & Mrs. Walter Thomas
Washington, DC

Mrs. Bernice Toliver & Family
Austin, TX

Rev. Robert F. Tywoniak
Fort Lauderdale, FL

Mr. Donald Wade
Baton Rouge, LA

Dr. & Mrs. Leon Weaver
Bowie, MD

Mrs. Mary Westbrook & Family
San Francisco, CA

The Honorable & Mrs. Horace Wheatley
Piedmont, CA

Mr. & Mrs. Curley & Annette Williams
Sarasota, FL

Mr. & Mrs. Benjamin Williams
Fort Lauderdale, FL

Dr. & Mrs. Spencer Wilson
Chicago, IL